Published by Macat International Ltd
24:13 Coda Centre, 189 Munster Road, London SW6 6AW.

Distributed exclusively by Routledge
2 Park Square, Milton Park, Abingdon, Oxon OX14 4RN
711 Third Avenue, New York, NY 10017, USA

Routledge is an imprint of the Taylor & Francis Group, an informa business

www.macat.com
info@macat.com

Cataloguing in Publication Data
A catalogue record for this book is available from the British Library.
Library of Congress Cataloguing-in-Publication Data is available upon request.
Cover illustration: Kim Thompson

ISBN 978-1-912302-04-8 (hardback)
ISBN 978-1-912128-52-5 (paperback)
ISBN 978-1-912128-29-7 (e-book)

Notice
The information in this book is designed to orientate readers of the work under analysis,
to elucidate and contextualise its key ideas and themes, and to aid in the development
of critical thinking skills. It is not meant to be used, nor should it be used, as a
substitute for original thinking or in place of original writing or research. References and
notes are provided for informational purposes and their presence does not constitute
endorsement of the information or opinions therein. This book is presented solely for
educational purposes. It is sold on the understanding that the publisher is not engaged
to provide any scholarly advice. The publisher has made every effort to ensure that
this book is accurate and up-to-date, but makes no warranties or representations with
regard to the completeness or reliability of the information it contains. The information
and the opinions provided herein are not guaranteed or warranted to produce particular
results and may not be suitable for students of every ability. The publisher shall not be
liable for any loss, damage or disruption arising from any errors or omissions, or from
the use of this book, including, but not limited to, special, incidental, consequential or
other damages caused, or alleged to have been caused, directly or indirectly, by the
information contained within.

MACAT

An Analysis of

E.E. Evans-Pritchard's

Witchcraft, Oracles, and Magic among the Azande

Kitty Wheater

CONTENTS

THE MACAT LIBRARY

The Macat Library is a series of unique academic explorations of seminal works in the humanities and social sciences – books and papers that have had a significant and widely recognised impact on their disciplines. It has been created to serve as much more than just a summary of what lies between the covers of a great book. It illuminates and explores the influences on, ideas of, and impact of that book. Our goal is to offer a learning resource that encourages critical thinking and fosters a better, deeper understanding of important ideas.

Each publication is divided into three Sections: Influences, Ideas, and Impact. Each Section has four Modules. These explore every important facet of the work, and the responses to it.

This Section-Module structure makes a Macat Library book easy to use, but it has another important feature. Because each Macat book is written to the same format, it is possible (and encouraged!) to cross-reference multiple Macat books along the same lines of inquiry or research. This allows the reader to open up interesting interdisciplinary pathways.

To further aid your reading, lists of glossary terms and people mentioned are included at the end of this book (these are indicated by an asterisk [*] throughout) – as well as a list of works cited.

Macat has worked with the University of Cambridge to identify the elements of critical thinking and understand the ways in which six different skills combine to enable effective thinking.
Three allow us to fully understand a problem; three more give us the tools to solve it. Together, these six skills make up the **PACIER** model of critical thinking. They are:

ANALYSIS – understanding how an argument is built
EVALUATION – exploring the strengths and weaknesses of an argument
INTERPRETATION – understanding issues of meaning

CREATIVE THINKING – coming up with new ideas and fresh connections
PROBLEM-SOLVING – producing strong solutions
REASONING – creating strong arguments

To find out more, visit **WWW.MACAT.COM.**

CRITICAL THINKING AND *WITCHCRAFT, ORACLES AND MAGIC AMONG THE AZANDE*

Primary critical thinking skill: INTERPRETATION
Secondary critical thinking skill: REASONING

The history of anthropology is, to a large extent, the history of differing modes of interpretation.

As anthropologists have long known, examining, analyzing and recording cultures in the quest to understand humankind as a whole is a vastly complex task, in which nothing can be achieved without careful and incisive interpretative work. Edward Evans-Pritchard's seminal 1937 *Witchcraft, Oracles, and Magic Among the Azande* is a model contribution to anthropology's grand interpretative project, and one whose success is based largely on its author's thinking skills. A major issue in anthropology at the time was the common assumption that the faiths and customs of other cultures appeared irrational or illogical when compared to the "civilized" and scientific beliefs of the western world.

Evans-Pritchard sought to challenge such definitions by embedding himself within a tribal culture in Africa – that of the Azande – and attempting to understand their beliefs in their proper contexts. By doing so, Evans-Pritchard proved just how vital context is to interpretation. Seen within their context, he was able to show, the beliefs of the Azande were far from irrational – and magic actually formed a coherent system that helped mould a functional community and society for the tribe. Evans-Pritchard's efforts to clarify meaning in this way have proved hugely influential, and have played a major part in guiding later generations of anthropologists from his day to ours.

ABOUT THE AUTHOR OF THE ORIGINAL WORK

Born in 1902, **Edward Evans-Pritchard** was one of the most important anthropologists of the twentieth century. He conducted research among the Azande people of the South Sudan before completing his PhD in 1927 at the London School of Economics, then a hothouse of British anthropological development. Evans-Pritchard's early career was hindered by a hostile relationship with his one-time mentor, Bronislaw Malinowski. However, his work on both the Azande, and later on their neighbors the Nuer, established his academic reputation, both in Britain and abroad. Evans-Pritchard's originality, engaging writing style, and detailed approach to fieldwork have consolidated his standing as a pioneer of his craft. He died at the age of 70 in 1973.

ABOUT THE AUTHOR OF THE ANALYSIS

Kitty Wheater is a PhD candidate in anthropology at the University of Oxford, where her work draws on the anthropology of ethics, embodiment, and new social/religious movements to develop an ethnography of intentional personhood and embodied practice.

ABOUT MACAT

GREAT WORKS FOR CRITICAL THINKING

Macat is focused on making the ideas of the world's great thinkers accessible and comprehensible to everybody, everywhere, in ways that promote the development of enhanced critical thinking skills.

It works with leading academics from the world's top universities to produce new analyses that focus on the ideas and the impact of the most influential works ever written across a wide variety of academic disciplines. Each of the works that sit at the heart of its growing library is an enduring example of great thinking. But by setting them in context – and looking at the influences that shaped their authors, as well as the responses they provoked – Macat encourages readers to look at these classics and game-changers with fresh eyes. Readers learn to think, engage and challenge their ideas, rather than simply accepting them.

'Macat offers an amazing first-of-its-kind tool for interdisciplinary learning and research. Its focus on works that transformed their disciplines and its rigorous approach, drawing on the world's leading experts and educational institutions, opens up a world-class education to anyone.'

Andreas Schleicher
Director for Education and Skills, Organisation for Economic Co-operation and Development

'Macat is taking on some of the major challenges in university education … They have drawn together a strong team of active academics who are producing teaching materials that are novel in the breadth of their approach.'

Prof Lord Broers,
former Vice-Chancellor of the University of Cambridge

'The Macat vision is exceptionally exciting. It focuses upon new modes of learning which analyse and explain seminal texts which have profoundly influenced world thinking and so social and economic development. It promotes the kind of critical thinking which is essential for any society and economy.
This is the learning of the future.'

Rt Hon Charles Clarke, former UK Secretary of State for Education

'The Macat analyses provide immediate access to the critical conversation surrounding the books that have shaped their respective discipline, which will make them an invaluable resource to all of those, students and teachers, working in the field.'

Professor William Tronzo, University of California at San Diego

WAYS IN TO THE TEXT

KEY POINTS

- Edward Evans-Pritchard (1902–73) was a British anthropologist.* Anthropology is the study of human social and cultural life.

- Published in 1937, *Witchcraft, Oracles, and Magic among the Azande* argues that "primitive" belief systems are just as logical as "modern" versions, but form in different cultural and social conditions.

- Witchcraft was the first in-depth anthropological text about the sociology of knowledge* (the study of the ways in which social and cultural factors structure individual perception, experience, and action).

Who Was Edward E. Evans-Pritchard?

Edward Evans-Pritchard, the author of *Witchcraft, Oracles, and Magic among the Azande* (1937), was born to an Anglican* family in the British county of Sussex in 1902. Anglicanism is a Protestant tradition within Christianity comprising the Church of England and allied Churches. While studying history at Oxford University he became interested in anthropology. After graduating, Evans-Pritchard left Oxford to study the subject at the London School of Economics,* where he was influenced by the pioneering anthropologist Bronislaw Malinowski,* despite their difficult working relationship.[1] Another

British anthropologist, Charles Seligman,* became Evans-Pritchard's mentor. Seligman had worked in the Southern Sudan area of northeastern Africa and Evans-Pritchard became interested in the Azande* people of this region, leaving for the Sudan himself in 1926. He published *Witchcraft* in 1937, though it did not attract much attention when it first appeared. Meanwhile Evans-Pritchard moved on to study the Nuer* people of the Sudan. After World War II* broke out in 1939, he left England to serve in Africa.[2]

In the 1930s Evans-Pritchard moved between academic posts in Egypt and the UK before taking up a permanent position at the University of Oxford in 1946. Anthropological interest in witchcraft*—recognized in Azande society as the ability to intentionally cause harm to someone else through supernatural methods—grew again in the 1950s, by which time Evans-Pritchard had become an important professor. During his career at Oxford he made a significant contribution to twentieth-century British anthropology, while focusing on graduate teaching and research, and was much loved by his doctoral students.[3]

Today, Evans-Pritchard is best remembered for his early works, including *Witchcraft* and *The Nuer*. Anthropologists remember him because he insisted on studying the beliefs of so-called "primitive" peoples on their own terms.

What Does *Witchcraft, Oracles, and Magic among the Azande* Say?

In Evans-Pritchard's time, the first half of the twentieth century, the Azande were a small-scale agricultural and hunter-gatherer* people in the Southern Sudan of northeastern Africa. *Witchcraft* argues that their belief system is logical and coherent.[4] In particular, it claims that it is equally as logical as "civilized" belief.

Evans-Pritchard argues that though witches,* oracles,* and magic* did not exist in the real world, the Azande nevertheless constructed a coherent belief system on the premise of their existence. For the Azande, the meanings of these terms are as follows:

- Witches: persons, usually considered of bad character, who intentionally or not send witchcraft-substance* (the substance found in the intestines that identifies a witch) to harm others.
- Oracles: unbiased authorities from which the Azande could seek answers, especially concerning the identity of witches.
- Magic: the use of substances, language, or action to bring about a change through supernatural forces; for the Azande, magic was used in revenge to inflict harm on witches.

The Azande believed that witches were real and could act invisibly in daily life. They identified witches by questioning the oracles and providing the names of people they suspected. When they discovered who the witch was, they created vengeance magic to protect themselves. Evans-Pritchard argues that this sequence of events is logical. Each step makes as much sense as any European choice when confronted with misfortune. This belief system protected an individual Zande* (the singular of Azande) by providing him or her with options. It also protected the whole of Azande society by ensuring that bad deeds would not go unpunished. This meant that Azande belief helped to support the social and moral order.

Evans-Pritchard argues that witchcraft beliefs are not unusual or threatening elements of Azande life but are, rather, everyday aspects of social and moral conduct.[5] This means that witchcraft beliefs support ordinary interactions in daily life. Among the Azande, belief in witchcraft encouraged good neighborliness. The possibility that an acquaintance was a witch made it good practice to behave well toward everybody, as a matter of course.

This was an important argument in anthropology at the time. Anthropologists and philosophers thought that "primitive" peoples were not as logical as "modern" peoples.[6] They believed that "primitive" societies would eventually evolve and become more sophisticated, and this affected the ways in which colonial* authorities (those from foreign lands who had invaded, occupied, and controlled a country) treated traditional societies in Africa. These authorities considered that their own home societies were more evolved, and so believed this gave them the right to exert their own power over peoples such as the Azande. Evans-Pritchard argued that this was not the case. In particular, he insisted that colonial authorities should not try to destroy "primitive" beliefs.[7] As a historian and anthropologist, Evans-Pritchard saw the importance of traditional beliefs and customs. *Witchcraft* attempts to document these customs for future generations.

Evans-Pritchard's conclusions show that he was a humanist,* a man who valued and respected all people. This comes across in the level of detail and personal anecdote in his work. There has been a resurgence of humanism with liberal thinking in recent decades, which means that *Witchcraft* continues to have an impact on humanist ideas for government policy abroad. It is also still widely read in the discipline of anthropology.

Witchcraft first appeared in 1937, without much impact.[8] This soon changed, however, and the work was abridged and republished in 1976. According to the academic search engine Google Scholar, scholars have cited a synopsis of the work over four thousand times. *Witchcraft* was and is an innovative text in the anthropology of Africa. It opened up several subject areas in medical anthropology* (the study of medical or health-related domains of social and culture life) and the anthropology of knowledge.* It also created academic debate about the contribution of anthropologists to colonial authority.[9]

Why Does *Witchcraft, Oracles, and Magic among the Azande* Matter?

Evans-Pritchard's study of Azande belief contains many extremely important lessons. It demonstrates the value of paying close attention to controversial topics. Religious belief continues to be a source of contention in society today. Division between "us" and "them" often occurs because of differing beliefs. This division creates social and political tension, sometimes with catastrophic results. Evans-Pritchard's work tried to rewrite the basic Western understanding of "other" peoples. It demonstrates curiosity, which is a guiding principle in scientific study. This protects both the natural and social sciences*— the study of human society and relationships—against any tendency to prejudge.

Witchcraft also encourages students to move out of the library and into the real world. Evans-Pritchard spent 20 months living with the Azande to write *Witchcraft*. Since the early twentieth century, anthropology has emphasized the importance of first-hand, close-up observation. *Witchcraft* provides a lesson in how to develop theory from fact, rather than the other way around.

The book also reminds the reader that *people* are the subjects of social science. The natural and social sciences develop general laws about the behaviors and properties of material or persons. Evans-Pritchard was interested in anthropological laws, but he was *more* interested in people.[10] People behave in ways that are not always expected by social scientists. *Witchcraft* shows that when people behave unpredictably, it is because the general law is not quite right. In the social sciences, critical thinkers need both to follow the people and to prove the hypothesis*—an explanation made based on available evidence, or with the expectation of discovering particular evidence.

Witchcraft also provides a helpful route into thinking about the ethics of researching human subjects. Evans-Pritchard's use of Azande informants*—the anthropological term for someone who is a source of information on the social or cultural practices and ideas of a group—is still controversial today. Is it right to gain information in this way? Is it acceptable to disrupt situations to learn more about them? *Witchcraft* raises questions about the relationship between ethics and knowledge. Are our findings scientific if we've used unethical methods?

Finally, *Witchcraft* is a lesson about complexity. It shows that the various components of a belief system interact in many different ways. A number of rules condition those interactions. The rules themselves operate at many levels: moral, social, scientific, and political. This complexity means that small changes can have unexpected consequences. If *Witchcraft* teaches that beliefs are complex, it also explains that they are dynamic, constantly changing, and evolving.[11]

NOTES

1 Christopher Morton, "Evans-Pritchard and Malinowski: The Roots of a Complex Relationship," *History of Anthropology Newsletter* 34, no. 2 (2007): 10–14.

2 J. A. Barnes, "Edward Evans-Pritchard: 1902–1973," *Proceedings of the British Academy* 73 (1987): 447–90.

3 Mary Douglas, *Edward Evans-Pritchard* (London: Fontana, 1980).

4 Edward Evans-Pritchard, *Witchcraft, Oracles, and Magic among the Azande* (Oxford: Clarendon Press, 1976), 16.

5 Evans-Pritchard, *Witchcraft*, 48.

6 Lucien Lévy-Bruhl, *How Natives Think,* trans. Lilian A. Clare (Princeton: Princeton University Press, 1985).

7 Edward Evans-Pritchard, "Witchcraft," *Africa* 8, no. 4 (1935): 417–22.

8 Douglas, *Evans-Pritchard*, 116.

9 Talal Asad, ed., *Anthropology and the Colonial Encounter* (London: Ithaca Press, 1973).

10 Meyer Fortes, "An Anthropologist's Apprenticeship," *Annual Review of Anthropology* 7 (1978): 6.

11 Mary Douglas, "Thirty Years after Witchcraft, Oracles and Magic," in *Witchcraft Confessions and Accusations,* ed. Mary Douglas (London: Tavistock Publications, 1970), xiv.

SECTION 1
INFLUENCES

MODULE 1
THE AUTHOR AND THE HISTORICAL CONTEXT

KEY POINTS

- *Witchcraft, Oracles, and Magic among the Azande* was published in 1937. It was an innovative text in the history of anthropology.*

- Evans-Pritchard's formative time at the London School of Economics* played a key role in his construction of the text.

- British colonialism* in the Southern Sudan was an important historical context for much of Evans-Pritchard's work.

Why Read This Text?

Anthropologists still read Edward Evans-Pritchard's *Witchcraft, Oracles, and Magic among the Azande* (1937) for several reasons:

- It is a classic text in the anthropology of Africa, capturing traditional practices and beliefs in a small-scale African society on the cusp of colonial change.

- It made a substantial contribution to anthropological knowledge. This impact was partly made in its own day, but it was also felt particularly in the 1950s onward, as scholars homed in on the topic of witchcraft* (here, the inherited capacity to do intentional harm to another person by supernatural means) and its relationship to social change.

- *Witchcraft's* central arguments—that Azande* belief was internally logical, and that belief in witchcraft supported the social and moral order—were innovative in 1937, while still understandable in the context of theories of the time.

> **❝ I should make it clear at this point that I am not, and never have been clever. ❞**
>
> Edward Evans-Pritchard, "Genesis of a Social Anthropologist: An Autobiographical Note"

Today, *Witchcraft* is recommended to students as an important text in the history of theory and practice in anthropology. Evans-Pritchard's rich and carefully considered writing is also considered an example of good style. As topics of interest have come full circle in the discipline, his text perhaps appeals to modern sensibilities that are less determined to make anthropology a dry science. In the posthumous 1976 edition of *Witchcraft,* he wrote: "I find the usual account of field-research so boring as often to be unreadable—kinship systems, political systems, ritual systems, every sort of system, structure and function, but little flesh and blood … If this is romanticism and sentimentality I accept those terms."[1] Evans-Pritchard was known for a level of human interest in his work that today, despite aspects that have inevitably dated, renders *Witchcraft* a surprisingly modern read.

Author's Life
Edward Evans-Pritchard was born in Sussex in 1902. Privately educated, he received a second-class degree in history at the University of Oxford, where he read contemporary studies of "primitive" cultures by the anthropologists Edward Tylor* and James Frazer* and became interested in the relatively new discipline of anthropology. In 1924 he moved to the London School of Economics (LSE) to study under the pioneering anthropologists Charles Seligman* and Bronislaw Malinowski.* In 1927 he completed his PhD thesis on witchcraft and magic* among the Azande, a small-scale agricultural people in the Southern Sudan region of northeastern Africa. In subsequent years, he held academic posts at the LSE and the Egyptian University of Cairo,*

and post–World War II* at the University of Oxford, where he was appointed professor in 1946 and became integral to the rise of its prestigious anthropology department.

Evans-Pritchard's work on the Azande, first published in 1937, and his later studies of their neighbors, the Nuer,* established his academic career as one of the foremost British anthropologists of the twentieth century. Yet it is worth noting that his early career was tumultuous— his fieldwork* (conducting long-term social scientific investigation among human societies) was repeatedly interrupted by illness or political turmoil, and his early job prospects were hindered by his hostile relationship with Malinowski, his one-time mentor.

Evans-Pritchard's intellectual biography is one of creative fusion between theistic* (religious) inclinations, intense social-scientific curiosity, and a vibrant personality. The Christian son of an Anglican* clergyman, Evans-Pritchard's understanding of the factual "incorrectness" of mystical* views—that is, experiences that go beyond physical reality—permeated his early work, but his own religious inclination probably made him sympathetic to the study of belief in an increasingly secular* intellectual climate (one in which it is felt that the state and other political institutions and practices should be kept separate from religious bodies).

The renowned British philosopher and anthropologist Ernest Gellner* described Evans-Pritchard as an "intellectually restless, ever-questing, skeptical Hamlet."*[2] The short memoir written by J. A. Barnes,* of the University of Cambridge, portrays him as a lively if temperamental figure,[3] while to British social anthropologist Mary Douglas* and his other doctoral students, "EP" was much loved.[4]

Author's Background

Evans-Pritchard conducted his fieldwork for *Witchcraft* in a southern region of the Sudan, administered at the time as an Anglo-Egyptian colony. His credentials as a highly educated English anthropologist helped him access the region, and the LSE's Charles Seligman, upon whose previous research in the area he hoped to build, also recommended him.

The richness of Evans-Pritchard's Anglo-Egyptian government-sponsored work in the Sudan among the Azande and the Nuer reflects the ambivalent relationship between anthropology and colonialism in the early to mid-twentieth century. Talal Asad* of the City University of New York has argued that anthropology in the interwar period—a discipline that then defined itself as the study of "primitive" peoples—was possible only because the colonial power dynamic enabled the safety of lone European fieldworkers among subjugated peoples.[5] In contrast, the British social anthropologist Jack Goody* has argued that professional anthropologists (rather than colonial officers who had completed a "crash course" in anthropology) were frequently at odds with colonial authorities.[6] "Social anthropology" focuses on the better understanding of institutions and conventions such as law, custom, exchange, status, and economy.

The production of *Witchcraft* suggests that there is some truth in both positions. Colonial backing was an equally mixed blessing in Evans-Pritchard's anthropological career—for example, in 1930 he arrived among the Nuer to considerable hostility because of recent government intervention in the area. Throughout his life, Evans-Pritchard's dialogue with colonial interests promoted intellectual analysis rather than interference, urging missionaries* and colonial administrators to avoid destroying the beliefs of subjugated peoples.[7] However, in his ethnography* (written text detailing the findings and analysis of an anthropological study), there is barely a whisper of any political climate. His detailed accounts of Azande belief and customs in *Witchcraft* suggest a commitment to social scientific evidence, free as far as possible from political agendas.

NOTES

1   Edward Evans-Pritchard, *Witchcraft, Oracles, and Magic among the Azande* (Oxford: Clarendon Press, 1976), 254.

2   Ernest Gellner, introduction to *A History of Anthropological Thought*, by Edward Evans-Pritchard (London: Faber and Faber, 1981).

3   J. A Barnes, "Edward Evans-Pritchard: 1902–1973," *Proceedings of the British Academy* 73 (1987): 447–90.

4   Mary Douglas, *Edward Evans-Pritchard* (London: Fontana, 1980).

5   Talal Asad, ed., *Anthropology and the Colonial Encounter* (London: Ithaca Press, 1973).

6   Jack Goody, *The Domestication of the Savage Mind* (Cambridge: Cambridge University Press, 1977).

7   Edward Evans-Pritchard, "Witchcraft," *Africa* 8, no. 4 (1935): 417–22.

ACADEMIC CONTEXT

KEY POINTS

- Before the pioneering work of Evans-Pritchard and his contemporaries, early anthropology* was interested in the difference between "primitive" and "modern" man.

- "Evolutionists"* thought that primitive cultures were less evolved than modern ones, while the subsequent "functionalists"* believed that primitive cultures functioned well on their own terms.

- Evans-Pritchard was basically a functionalist, and left behind the evolutionist search for the "origins" of religion.

The Work in its Context

Edward Evans-Pritchard's *Witchcraft, Oracles, and Magic among the Azande* is interesting for its position in the history of anthropological writing.

In the late nineteenth and early twentieth centuries, anthropology was preoccupied with a central question: In what way was "primitive, irrational" man different from "modern, scientific" man?[1] The field's dominant theory was one of evolutionism: the idea that cultures existed on a linear spectrum of development, from primitivism to scientific modernity. According to this theory, cultures were either more or less evolved than others, rather than developing in individual ways and on different trajectories (paths). It was thought that the investigation of "primitive" and "less evolved" peoples could reveal basic facts of human social life and thereby create a human science—that is, anthropology.

> 66 It is extraordinary that anyone could have thought
> it worth while to speculate about what might have
> been the origin of some custom or belief, when there
> is absolutely no means of discovering, in the absence of
> historical evidence, what was its origin. 99
>
> Edward Evans-Pritchard, *Theories of Primitive Religion*

The cultures of "primitive" or "savage" peoples such as the Azande* were thought to directly mirror those of modern Western Europe's forebears. The former were considered "pre-logical"—even incomprehensible—while the latter demonstrated post-Enlightenment* rationality (the Enlightenment was the philosophical movement in the eighteenth century that celebrated the power of rationality). Key points of difference such as a belief in magic* and animism*—faith in the existence of spiritual properties in nonhuman things or beings, such as rocks, trees, or animals—were a critical focus of investigation during this period, because they appeared to distinguish the primitive from the modern mind.

When Edward Evans-Pritchard began his career, British anthropologists of the 1920s and 1930s assumed that a "human science" was possible. They began to shift from evolutionism toward an early form of functionalism (the theory that every aspect of social life exists to preserve the existence of the social order). They argued that mutually reinforcing relationships existed between the component parts of societies, rendering an internally coherent whole, and that evidence for this could be obtained through rigorous fieldwork* (long-term participant-observation* among the peoples under study, during which the anthropologist immerses him or herself in the society being observed).

Whereas evolutionists rarely conducted primary fieldwork, the functionalist project was built on the necessity of empirical methods:

that is, methods that emphasized observation and verifiability over theory. This meant that Evans-Pritchard and his contemporaries challenged the distinction made between prelogical and logical societies. Anthropologists Jonathan Spencer* and Alan Barnard* describe this period's intellectual rifts as partly political, typified by "younger practitioners determined to discredit their elders' theoretical commitments."[2] But in *Witchcraft,* and also in his subsequent academic career, Evans-Pritchard demonstrated his own intellectual commitment to research based on empirical grounds, rather than those of academic politics.

Overview of the Field

As anthropology underwent a theoretical transition from favoring evolutionism to functionalism, scholars investigating the nature of so-called primitive minds tried to construct a sociology of knowledge.* This was a highly interdisciplinary* field (that is, it drew on the aims and methods of several different academic disciplines), with contributions from psychologists, philosophers, and anthropologists. At this stage, the problem of the function of religious belief within a society focused the debate.[3] This superseded previous work such as that of social anthropologist James Frazer*—despite its own pioneering qualities, Frazer's work had the primary purpose of debunking, rather than explaining, the central tenets of religious belief.

The emphasis on religious belief during the period arguably responded to the challenges of colonialism* after World War I.* Displays of power and assertions of superiority were not enough to enact authority over peoples who had very different religious beliefs and practices. For example, the translator and anthropologist Eva Gillies,* who abridged *Witchcraft* for its popular 1976 edition, comments that in the 1920s the Azande were moved from a dispersed pattern of settlement into close-knit settlements along major roads.[4] For the Azande, witchcraft* was more easily practiced at a close distance. Their unwillingness to live closely to one another remained a mysterious source of frustration and upset for colonial authorities, despite the ostensible health benefits gained from the easier close-quarters monitoring of sleeping sickness. When "primitive" societies failed to adapt happily as expected when a "modern" order was imposed from outside, anthropologists began to question the mechanisms of social evolution, and to seek to understand the functioning of belief on its own terms.

Academic Influences

Evans-Pritchard wrote in a well-established tradition of social anthropology of religion, but pioneered, along with his one-time mentor Bronislaw Malinowski,* the functionalist fieldwork project. During his education, the seminal figures in the academic scholarship of religion had been Edward Tylor* and James Frazer. Tylor, considered by many to be the founding father of social anthropology, argued in the 1860s that thought, belief, habit, and tradition "survived" in contemporary primitive cultures from earlier stages of their culture.[5] Like many early anthropologists, he was most interested in the "origins" question: how aspects of religion and social life had developed in the first place. Tylor suggested that animism was the earliest form of religion. This identification of animism with "early" man led to the evolutionist theory of culture in the young field of anthropology, and assumptions that "primitive" peoples who believed in animism and magic belonged to less "evolved" forms of society.

James Frazer followed in Tylor's footsteps. A life-long secularist,* his search for the origins of religious tropes, or texts, served an agenda of debunking the truth behind the major religions. The historian of anthropology Robert Ackerman* argues that Frazer's seminal work *The Golden Bough* (1890) attacked classical religious thought and covertly criticized both primitive belief and a central doctrinal aspect of Christianity—the Resurrection.[6] Frazer adhered to Tylor's cultural evolutionism, arguing that primitive magic was inevitably supplanted by religion, which in turn gave way to rationalist* science ("rationalism" referring to a pursuit with rational ends and means). *Witchcraft* would leave the "origins" quest, and be motivated by new questions.

NOTES

1   Mary Douglas, *Edward Evans-Pritchard* (London: Fontana, 1980), 15.

2   Jonathan Spencer and Alan Bernard, "Functionalism," in *The Routledge Encyclopedia of Social and Cultural Anthropology* (London: Routledge, 2010); also "The Politics of Knowledge," accessed October 25, 2015, eBook Collection (EBSCOhost).

3   Douglas, *Evans-Pritchard*, 35.

4   Eva Gillies, introduction to *Witchcraft, Oracles, and Magic among the Azande*, by Edward Evans-Pritchard (Oxford: Clarendon Press, 1976), VIII.

5   Edward Tylor, "On the Survival of Savage Thought in Modern Civilization," *Proceedings of the Royal Institute* (1869).

6   Robert Ackerman, "Frazer, Sir James George (1854–1941)," Oxford Dictionary of National Biography (Oxford: Oxford University Press, 2004), accessed October 25, 2015, www.oxforddnb.com/view/article/33258.

MODULE 3
THE PROBLEM

KEY POINTS

- Post-Enlightenment* academics questioned why irrational religious beliefs existed.

- Evans-Pritchard was influenced by the work of the French sociologist Émile Durkheim* and the French philosopher Lucien Lévy-Bruhl,* who argued that religious beliefs were the collective constructions of fundamentally different mentalities. He was also influenced by Bronislaw Malinowski,* who argued that religious belief had a social "function."

- While Evans-Pritchard builds upon work by all of the debate's participants, he does not acknowledge them in *Witchcraft, Oracles, and Magic among the Azande.*

Core Question

In *Witchcraft, Oracles, and Magic among the Azande*, Edward Evans-Pritchard places his core anthropological* question within academia's broader debate into the formation of religious beliefs. He provides a twist on Bronislaw Malinowski's functionalist* investigations. If witchcraft* beliefs and practices are basically false, asks Evans-Pritchard, how do they come to be part of a society's belief system? And what purpose do they serve? These questions focused the debate very specifically on "primitive" religions that especially challenged Western sensibilities. They raised the possibility that beliefs had some kind of purpose in the present-day functioning of the society, and were not just relics from an older time.

This undercut the underlying assumptions of post-Enlightenment rationalism* in academia. The evolutionists* argued that primitive

> **❝** Witches, as the Azande conceive them, clearly cannot exist. **❞**
>
> Edward Evans-Pritchard, *Witchcraft, Oracles, and Magic among the Azande*

religious beliefs were objectively not "true": ghosts, witches, and spirits did not exist, and beliefs in these would eventually be replaced by rational science. Their assumption, that primitive religion was totally different from the working framework of natural sciences, had led to conclusions that primitive peoples were completely different from Europeans. This was despite the endurance of major world religions in European belief.

Evans-Pritchard wanted to look beyond the face value of these assumptions. He chose instead to investigate categories of belief that were considered "true" by peoples such as the Azande.* Understanding belief as a sociological fact, rather than as a natural truth (that is, as something that must be understood by considering the social context in which the belief is held without consideration of its truth or falsity), he looked for new answers as to how and why witchcraft beliefs formed and functioned within a society's present moment, rather than simply being "accepted" as historical artifacts.

The Participants

Evans-Pritchard was heavily influenced by the philosopher Lucien Lévy-Bruhl, who in turn drew upon the work of the sociologist Émile Durkheim. Durkheim argued that representations (roughly, symbols) and beliefs are formed collectively. This is an ongoing, back-and-forth construction of meaning, shaped both by the individual and by society as a whole.[1] Lévy-Bruhl agreed, and argued that primitive thought was actually a "mentality" that was quite different in essence from a Western, logical mentality. So the religious "collective representations"* (symbols with collective meaning to the members of a particular society) of the primitive mind would be incompatible with the Western mind, because their component parts "participated" together in a way that was not rational.[2] The participants in this debate therefore assumed, first, a collective nature to belief and, second, a dichotomy (division) of mentalities between the primitive and the rational.

Evans-Pritchard acknowledged his debts to French scholarship.[3] The British social anthropologist Mary Douglas* adds that in his research agenda he drew extensively upon interdisciplinary* (cross-discipline) contributions to the contemporary understanding of knowledge. She argues that he adopted the same vocabulary about selective principles of attention as the experimental psychologist Frederick Bartlett* (who used scientific methods to conduct research on the human mind and behavior). Bartlett argued that although the process of gaining knowledge is selective, as was widely accepted, this selectivity was always influenced by social experiences because human beings are social animals.[4]

Evans-Pritchard also acknowledged work by the philosopher Eugenio Rignano* on experience and selective attention.[5] Rignano argued that experiences such as hunger grab our attention not because our life is imminently threatened—a human being can survive for weeks without food. Instead, human perception substitutes the part (hunger) for the whole (starvation), attracting our attention so that action is taken long before starvation really threatens. Evans-Pritchard thought that social institutions, as well as human perception, might show similar processes of selective attention. These would support ongoing behavior that protected religious belief, rather than human nutrition.

The Contemporary Debate

Although Evans-Pritchard acknowledged some of the work that influenced him, in *Witchcraft* itself he does not mention contemporary debates or theorists of any kind. The book consists only of extensive ethnography* (that is, the findings of his anthropological study) and analysis of this on its own terms. This might be attributable to the ambivalence of Evans-Pritchard's experience during his studies at the London School of Economics* in the 1920s under Malinowski. The latter was critical of much of Evans-Pritchard's work, and personal animosity characterized much of their relationship. Yet Evans-Pritchard's functionalist approach and his fieldwork* in the Azande language suggest the influence of the older anthropologist, for whom both of these principles were vital. Evans-Pritchard specifically emphasized the importance of fieldwork: he famously described Lévy-Bruhl as an "armchair theorist."[6]

Malinowski's functionalist analysis of magic* (the ability to effect change through supernatural forces) was also an important precedent for *Witchcraft*. He argued that magic was used as a response to uncertainty and anxiety. He observed that in the Trobriand Islands* in Papua New Guinea, magical rites accompanied dangerous open-sea fishing, while lagoon fishing went unremarked. He thereby argued that magic had important *functions* in social life, and was not solely a relic of history, nor a pathology* (something at variance with the healthy norm) of illogical mentalities.[7] In the early 1930s, Evans-Pritchard did address his forebears directly outside *Witchcraft*, critiquing first Tylor and Frazer,[8] and then Lévy-Bruhl—but he did not mention Malinowski.[9]

NOTES

1   Émile Durkheim, *The Elementary Forms of Religious Life,* trans. Karen Fields (London: Free Press, 1995).

2   Lucien Lévy-Bruhl, *How Natives Think,* trans. Lilian A. Clare (Princeton: Princeton University Press, 1985), 52, 84, 121–3.

3   Edward Evans-Pritchard, "Lévy-Bruhl's Theory of Primitive Mentality," *Bulletin of the Faculty of Arts* 2 (University of Egypt, Cairo, 1934): 9.

4   Frederick Bartlett, *Psychology and Primitive Culture* (Cambridge: Cambridge University Press, 1923).

5   Evans-Pritchard, "Lévy-Bruhl," 18.

6   Edward Evans-Pritchard, *Theories of Primitive Religion* (Oxford: Clarendon Press, 1965), 81.

7   Bronislaw Malinowski, *Argonauts of the Western Pacific* (London: Routledge and Kegan Paul, 1922).

8   Edward Evans-Pritchard, "The Intellectualist (English) Interpretation of Magic," *Bulletin of the Faculty of Arts* 1 (University of Egypt, Cairo, 1933).

9   Evans-Pritchard, "Lévy-Bruhl."

MODULE 4
THE AUTHOR'S CONTRIBUTION

KEY POINTS

- Evans-Pritchard argues that witchcraft* beliefs have a function in the social structure and moral order of a society.

- The quality of his ethnographic* evidence, drawn from firsthand observation, makes his argument a major contribution to the field.

- His work directly builds on the questions, models, and methods of previous scholars, but his approach is deliberately curious and open-ended.

Author's Aims

Edward Evans-Pritchard's main aims in *Witchcraft, Oracles, and Magic among the Azande* were both descriptive and analytical. First, the text was an attempt to use ethnographic findings, where others had not, to methodically describe a system of thought and belief that seemed alien to most Europeans of his day. Indeed, this system of thought was fast disappearing in the Southern Sudan as a result of the pace of colonial* change. Second, Evans-Pritchard wanted to challenge the prevailing view—in academia and elsewhere—that there was a fundamental divide between "primitive" people and "civilized" people. *Witchcraft* was the beginning of a series of works that sought to communicate his views with concrete ethnographic examples.

The structure of *Witchcraft* demonstrates how Evans-Pritchard brought together both aspects of his intellectual agenda. The 1937 edition contained a large quantity of descriptive ethnographic writing. Some of this was cut for the (possibly more influential) 1976 abridged

> 66 A scientist takes the hypotheses of his predecessors and ... checks them by observation. By these means he selects what he finds to be valid in each hypothesis and works them into a coordinated system. He adds his own observations and inferences and these in turn serve as hypotheses till they are verified by independent workers, and are recognized as true by the consensus of specialized opinion. 99
>
> Edward Evans-Pritchard, "The Intellectualist (English) Interpretation of Magic"

edition. Evans-Pritchard first describes the mysterious aspects of Azande* religious thought, such as witch doctors* and "poison oracles";* and second, he consistently places these in the context of Azande society and cosmology* (in philosophy, inquiries into the laws of the universe). He therefore builds a case that ultimately realizes his intellectual aims, arguing that mystical beliefs directly support the social structure and moral order of a society.

Approach

The particular inventiveness of Evans-Pritchard's approach was his commitment to understanding the everyday context in which religious beliefs appear. A historian or other contemporary commentator might have observed the bigger social setting within which Azande life operated. It was a society in flux under colonial power, with its social organization and power structures eroding and changing. But Evans-Pritchard makes no mention of this in his approach to the study of the Azande; instead, through ethnographic method, he accesses his subject on a day-to-day, encounter-to-encounter level: the microsocial context.

Evans-Pritchard lived among the Azande in the Southern Sudan on and off between 1926 and 1930, staying in a settlement with a

Zande* servant named Kamanga.* He participated fully in daily life, taking copious notes. This followed Bronislaw Malinowski's* advocacy of the method of "participant-observation,"* the anthropological* method of spending long periods sharing in the social and cultural lives of other peoples, to increase the understanding of them and in order to analyze them scientifically. He consulted the poison oracle himself (who fed poison to chickens and asked them who is responsible for one's misfortune) and experienced sickness that the Azande attributed to witchcraft.[1] He sought to witness the chain of events resulting in an accusation of witchcraft, or the arrangement of a poison oracle.

Evans-Pritchard's analysis of micro-social context creates space both for human beings and social laws. Meyer Fortes,* his friend and colleague at the London School of Economics,* describes how with Evans-Pritchard "the sense that in the field one would be dealing with living people, with named, idiosyncratic individuals and not with abstract customs or patterns of social organization, came through more immediately than with Malinowski."[2]

Contribution in Context

As is the case with most young anthropologists, Evans-Pritchard borrowed his preliminary questions, concepts, models, and methods from other anthropologists, psychologists, and philosophers. The originality of his contribution arose from the peculiar combination of his theoretical approach and verifiable findings. While he did not at this point have a particular theoretical orientation within the anthropology of religion, he did have a particular stance in terms of the method he employed in his approach—he set an original precedent for fieldwork* that was hypothesis*-driven and inductive (that is, it used observation to generate a conclusion), rather than ideologically driven.

Prior to his work, the field of "primitive" study assumed that primitive peoples were less evolved than and inferior to "modern" peoples. Evans-Pritchard replaced these negative assumptions with alternative hypotheses: What if witchcraft beliefs were not socially destructive, but constructive? What if inconsistencies in primitive thought resulted from hidden, logical functions, rather than from intellectual failing? Unusually, he enacted this curiosity-driven approach by following the interests of his informants*—the people who provided him with information—in the field, rather than imposing prior agendas upon his findings: "I had no interest in witchcraft when I went to Zandeland,* but the Azande had; so I had to let myself be guided by them."[3] His findings produced the first extensive study of witchcraft belief and practice in a "primitive" culture—a major contribution to twentieth-century anthropology.

NOTES

1   Edward Evans-Pritchard, *Witchcraft, Oracles, and Magic among the Azande* (Oxford: Clarendon Press, 1976), 44–5.

2   Meyer Fortes, "An Anthropologist's Apprenticeship," *Annual Review of Anthropology* 7 (1978): 6.

3   Evans-Pritchard, *Witchcraft,* 242.

SECTION 2
IDEAS

MODULE 5
MAIN IDEAS

KEY POINTS

- In *Witchcraft, Oracles, and Magic among the Azande*, Evans-Pritchard's key themes are the nature of primitive minds, the function of religious belief, and the maintenance of the social and moral order.

- He argues that Azande* belief was internally rational, that there was nothing inherently primitive about their mentality, and that witchcraft* beliefs actually supported the moral order.

- His main ideas are presented in ethnographic* case studies—written accounts of anthropological fieldwork. These demonstrate rational Azande beliefs in action.

Key Themes

Edward Evans-Pritchard's overarching argument in *Witchcraft, Oracles, and Magic among the Azande* is that the Azande religious belief system is central to establishing and maintaining moral order in the Zandeland* region of Southern Sudan. The belief system itself is a coherent three-part structure made up of witchcraft, oracles,* and magic.* As a social scientist, Evans-Pritchard was not predominantly interested in disputing the truth of the belief system. Instead, he wished to identify what and whose purposes it served—a functionalist* approach that informed the various themes he identified in *Witchcraft*; this argument itself had important implications for the anthropology* of "primitive" peoples.

First, Evans-Pritchard notes that misfortune requires explanation and remedy in all societies. Where we might simply attribute misfortune to "bad luck," the Azande seek further investigation

> ❝ The Zande mind is logical and inquiring within the framework of its own culture and insists on the coherence of its own idiom. ❞
>
> Edward Evans-Pritchard, *Witchcraft, Oracles, and Magic among the Azande*

through questioning the oracle and making accusations of witchcraft. Second, much of the belief system itself is internally coherent. These first two themes speak to a common conclusion: the *rationality* of the Azande as a people, despite being "primitive."

Subsequent themes, building on these, contributed in particular to Evans-Pritchard's conclusion that witchcraft beliefs and practices conserved the moral and social order. First, by offering a means of identifying a perpetrator, the belief system offered accountability. This promoted good neighborliness: a person would try to avoid behaving disagreeably for fear of either being accused of witchcraft, or having others bewitch them. Second, the belief system contained loopholes. If one aspect threatened important tenets of the social order—for example, if an accusation of witchcraft was made against the Azande elite, threatening their social supremacy—other aspects could be used to keep this in place.

Exploring the Ideas

Evans-Pritchard's argument that the Azande belief system was rational was based largely on its logical system of cause and effect. Just as Westerners distinguished between *how* something happens and *why* it happens, so did the Azande. Evans-Pritchard used the following example: a person is sitting under a granary* on a hot day, the granary collapses, and the person suffers injuries. The factual processes through which this event occurred are as follows: first, people sit under granaries for shade on hot days; second, termites* eat away at the foundations of buildings. But it must be explained why, at that particular moment, with that particular person underneath, the granary collapsed. For the "why" of the event, accountability is located not in the concept of "bad luck," or even today in perhaps a more litigious "health and safety negligence" factor. Instead it is attributed to witchcraft: a person wished some mishap upon the unfortunate shade-seeker.[1]

This led Evans-Pritchard to his next main theme: that a belief system of witchcraft, oracles, and magic supports the moral order by ensuring accountability. The injured party or his or her relatives can turn to the oracles to establish which person has bewitched them, causing the granary to collapse. The poison oracle* is consulted by acquiring chickens and feeding them poison in turn, asking the oracle whether this man or that man is to blame. If the man named is the witch, the chicken will die. If not, the chicken will recover. The injured party continues the inquiry until a named person is implicated.[2] If the witch does not desist with a verbal warning, the aggrieved person or his or her kinsmen enact vengeance-magic to discourage the witch.[3] Evans-Pritchard observed that this enabled accountability for all issues of misfortune that might lie outside the realm of criminal or civil law. This accountability in turn promoted good neighborliness, out of fear of the consequences of an accusation of witchcraft.[4]

Evans-Pritchard noted that the inconsistencies within the belief system also promoted social order. For example, the moral function of witchcraft appeared to depend on its *uncertainty* and *invisibility*: one could not know whether one's neighbor or trading partner was a witch, so one behaved well. Yet witchcraft was also known to be hereditary* (passed through generations of the same family), which gave it a kind of certainty. It was demonstrated by witchcraft-substance,* which—if a deceased Azande were a witch—was found in the intestines at autopsy.*[5] This meant that over time, with sufficient cases of witchcraft, one should have been able to discern which lines of descent in Azande society contained witchcraft: it should not have been uncertain at all. Indeed, the *avongara** (Azande aristocracy—people of high social status) were known to be hereditarily free from witchcraft-substance.[6] This was an internal contradiction, but the loophole actually protected the social hierarchy: it meant that a commoner could not accuse an aristocrat of witchcraft. Even inconsistencies in belief therefore had a social and moral function in Azande society.

Language and Expression

The vocabulary of *Witchcraft* is distinctive. Evans-Pritchard often used the vocabulary of "savages" in his other work, even when he was refuting claims made by others about their nature of mind. "It is … a mistake to say that savages perceive mystically* or that their perception is mystical," he wrote in 1934.[7] However, *Witchcraft* is generally free from this pejorative language, even in its 1937 edition. When Evans-Pritchard concludes that one could never really "become" a Zande* or Nuer,* he still resists the temptation to dismiss the idea by using the derogatory words "primitive" or "savage."[8] He seems to have avoided any loaded vocabulary that would have alluded to the often moralizing, rather than social scientific, contemporary discourse on "primitive" peoples ("discourse" here signifies, roughly, a combination of language and discussion on a specific subject). His conclusion, that Azande belief was logical and functional in the context of its society, is therefore subtly reinforced by the respectful nature of his language.

Finally, the coolly observational tone of *Witchcraft* is consistent with the authoritative style of much subsequent twentieth-century anthropology. Evans-Pritchard frequently writes as if he considers himself a removed observer, and any reflective consideration of what he might not have noticed or been able to access as a white male Westerner does not appear in the main body of the text. An appendix on fieldwork* appears in the 1976 edition as an add-on, rather than as something integral to the kind of findings he was able to produce.[9] Evans–Pritchard's methodological* style—the systematic approach to gathering and analyzing information he employed—preserves the impression of *Witchcraft* as an authoritative social scientific work.

NOTES

1   Edward Evans-Pritchard, *Witchcraft, Oracles, and Magic among the Azande* (Oxford: Clarendon Press, 1976), 24.

2   Evans-Pritchard, *Witchcraft,* 39–40.

3   Evans-Pritchard, *Witchcraft,* 55, 64, 66, 97.

4   Evans-Pritchard, *Witchcraft,* 52.

5   Evans-Pritchard, *Witchcraft,* 2.

6   Evans-Pritchard, *Witchcraft,* 58.

7   Edward Evans-Pritchard, "Lévy-Bruhl's Theory of Primitive Mentality," *Bulletin of the Faculty of Arts* 2 (University of Egypt, Cairo, 1934): 29.

8   Evans-Pritchard, *Witchcraft,* 243.

9   Evans-Pritchard, *Witchcraft,* 240.

MODULE 6
SECONDARY IDEAS

KEY POINTS

- Evans-Pritchard argues that witchcraft* is not a special or terrifying part of Azande* belief, but an ordinary part of everyday moral and social life.

- The argument emerges more clearly in the 1937 edition of *Witchcraft, Oracles, and Magic among the Azande*—it was overlooked in the better-known 1976 abridged publication of the book.

- This idea has been rediscovered in the recent anthropology* of everyday knowledge, action, and morality.

Other Ideas

The argument of *Witchcraft, Oracles, and Magic among the Azande* is so tightly woven that even Edward Evans-Pritchard's secondary ideas were important for his main thesis. His central idea, that witchcraft beliefs supported the functioning of the social and moral order, was linked to a further observation that scholars have argued was a key part of the 1937 edition and was overlooked in 1976: that witchcraft was an ordinary part of daily life, and therefore that religious belief was intrinsically linked to (and perhaps no different from) everyday social and moral reasoning.

This was an important idea, because supernatural belief such as witchcraft had been analytically ring-fenced by scholars as something that was activated only in times of conflict—a "special case," showing society going "wrong." As the British social anthropologist Mary Douglas* later commented, Evans-Pritchard's observation that "conflict" was actually an ordinary part of the social order was an

> ❝ Witchcraft beliefs ... embrace a system of values which regulate human conduct. ❞
>
> Edward Evans-Pritchard, *Witchcraft, Oracles, and Magic among the Azande*

important one for anthropology: "By accepting conflict as a normal part of any social system we have developed a more realistic model."[1] Evans-Pritchard's idea therefore subverted the contemporary understanding of witchcraft as a destructive force. Instead, he normalized the occurrence of such conflict. He made this a sign of a healthily self-regulating society, whose systems contain checks and balances that activate regularly to ensure social order.

Exploring the Ideas

Evans-Pritchard argues that the everyday immediacy of witchcraft was shown by the time-specific way that Azande consulted the oracle:* "A man never asks the oracles ... whether a certain man is a witch. He asks whether at the moment this man is bewitching him."[2] The Azande understood witchcraft to be operating in this moment, right now. They therefore determined moral accountability on an immediate, everyday basis, rather than considering it something conceptual or structural that was separate from their daily lives.

Evans-Pritchard clearly sets out this relationship between witchcraft, the social and moral order, and everyday social and moral behavior. He argues that belief in witchcraft stepped into the moral gap where the Azande's notions of civil and criminal liability ended. In Christian belief, he says, moral codes are judged by God, who acts as "the guardian of moral law."[3] In Azande society, these codes are sustained by the collective construction of the power of witchcraft, oracles, and magic. These are particularly used in the containment of everyday difficult emotions and misconduct such as hatred, greed, jealousy, and dishonesty. Witches are believed to bewitch people against whom they hold a grudge: witchcraft is an invisible act of vengeance. People who are *seen* to behave as good, moral citizens are therefore far less likely to be accused of witchcraft; meanwhile, those who commonly display unpleasant character traits can gain reputations as likely witches.[4] Taken to the extreme, an allegation of witchcraft might result in the perpetrator's death, so Evans-Pritchard argues that fear of accusation created the motivation to behave well.

In *Witchcraft*, belief in witchcraft works to ensure everyday moral decorum (civility and propriety) in the opposite direction as well: not only do people wish to avoid being accused of witchcraft, they also want to avoid unduly antagonizing anyone who might be a witch and harm them. The physical characteristics of a witch are not externally observable: "witchcraft-substance,"* the hereditary* matter that demonstrates that a person is a witch, is stored in the intestines. This makes it impossible to be certain of your neighbors: "It is … better to earn no man's enmity since hatred is the motive in every act of witchcraft," comments Evans-Pritchard. It is a pragmatic, everyday necessity to keep relations amicable with everybody.[5] This norm of moral behavior is demonstrated by the fact that Azande who were accused of witchcraft frequently pleaded that they acted unintentionally. As far as they were concerned, their intention was to behave well despite grudges that might arise, and if they bewitched a neighbor it was beyond their control.[6]

Overlooked

At first, Evans-Pritchard's idea that witchcraft had an ordinary, everyday, and constructive function in the social and moral order of the Azande was overlooked. The notion that witchcraft beliefs were oppressive and painful endured through much of the rest of twentieth-century anthropology. Mary Douglas argued in 1980 that what the text has to say about the relationship between knowledge and action had also been overlooked, despite the fact that this is a strong theme for Evans-Pritchard, who writes, "Azande experience feelings about witchcraft rather than ideas, for their intellectual concepts of it are weak and they know better what to do when attacked by it than how to explain it. Their response is action and not analysis."[7] Referencing "missionaries,"* people who travel with the intention of converting others to Christianity, Mary Douglas observed that in the case of contradictions arising within a belief system, "Somewhere reasoning has to come to an end ... Why are the people so certain that they are right and the missionary's story is wrong? Because they have to live and act: action proceeds upon decisions and decisions upon assumptions."[8]

Douglas's advocacy of anthropological investigation of the relationship between knowledge and action would in due course be fruitful in medical anthropology* of the 1990s and beyond.[9] Evans-Pritchard's interest in the limits of conceptual knowledge would also reemerge in later anthropology, in particular, that of the emotions.[10] Meanwhile, these ideas were overlooked, despite the fact that where Evans-Pritchard excelled was in witnessing the ordinary, everyday nature of thinking, believing, and doing.

NOTES

1 Mary Douglas, "Thirty Years after Witchcraft, Oracles and Magic," in *Witchcraft Confessions and Accusations*, ed. Mary Douglas (London: Tavistock Publications, 1970), xxiv.

2 Edward Evans-Pritchard, *Witchcraft, Oracles, and Magic among the Azande* (Oxford: Clarendon Press, 1976), 4.

3 Evans-Pritchard, *Witchcraft,* 51.

4 Evans-Pritchard, *Witchcraft,* 52.

5 Evans-Pritchard, *Witchcraft,* 55.

6 Evans-Pritchard, *Witchcraft,* 57.

7 Evans-Pritchard, *Witchcraft,* 31.

8   Mary Douglas, *Edward Evans-Pritchard* (London: Fontana, 1980), 37.

9   Margaret Lock and Patricia Kaufert, eds., *Pragmatic Women and Body Politics* (Cambridge: Cambridge University Press, 1998).

10 Catherine Lutz, "The Anthropology of Emotions," *Annual Review of Anthropology* 15 (1986): 405–36.

MODULE 7
ACHIEVEMENT

KEY POINTS

- With *Witchcraft, Oracles, and Magic among the Azande*, Evans-Pritchard successfully challenged the analytical division made by academics between "primitive" and "modern" minds.

- His original firsthand ethnographic* research among the Azande* people of South Sudan provided new evidence about the social function of belief.

- Evans-Pritchard's achievement was constrained by his lack of critical reflection on the larger structural and historical contexts of his research, and his own position within those contexts.

Assessing the Argument

In *Witchcraft, Oracles, and Magic among the Azande*, Edward Evans-Pritchard outlined a three-part belief system of witchcraft,* oracles,* and magic,* demonstrating how this system and the interactions among its constituent elements arose through the fabrication of the social and moral order. This was a major realization of Evans-Pritchard's attempts to comprehend "primitive" belief within what he termed "the coherence of its own idiom"[1]—roughly, the sense a belief makes in its particular context. As an early anthropologist* committed to understanding the thought of peoples very different from his own, the argument succeeded largely based on its foundation upon firsthand anthropological fieldwork.* His mentor, the British anthropologist Charles Seligman,* had conducted only survey research. This could not capture "primitive" belief at the in-depth level needed to challenge the dominant intellectual climate.

> ❝ Anyone can produce a new fact; the thing is to produce a new idea. ❞
>
> Edward Evans-Pritchard, *Witchcraft, Oracles, and Magic among the Azande*

Evans-Pritchard was committed to empirical research (research founded on evidence verifiable by observation), and from his perspective, his argument could be only as good as its evidence. His prolonged passages of ethnographic observation, many of which were cut from the text in the more popular 1976 edition of *Witchcraft*, testified to his notion of anthropological evidence itself. Evans-Pritchard's attention to microsocial context—the everyday unfolding of social and moral deportment in Azande life—was not only vital for his argument, but was also a major contribution to emerging functionalism* and its primary method, participant-observation.* Most importantly, Evans-Pritchard's questioning of the essentialist dichotomy (polar opposition) between "primitive" and "scientific" (European) mentalities was so influential that it has simply been taken for granted by subsequent generations of anthropologists. "Essentialism" is the belief that certain things are fundamentally different because of essential properties that define them.

Achievement in Context

Evans-Pritchard's intellectual achievement in the context of his time was considerable. In the 1920s and 1930s, the discipline of anthropology in Britain was in a process of evolution and uncertainty—it consisted of just a few pioneers, most of whom huddled round a seminar table at the London School of Economics.* Yet Evans-Pritchard produced an analysis that drew together and invited further interdisciplinary* contributions. Moreover, his study was based on the relatively new method of participant-observation. This required a personal commitment well beyond the "armchair anthropologists" of previous decades, and helped redefine the nature of anthropology. *Witchcraft* established new intellectual precedents concerning the study of religious belief, and, in particular, witchcraft. This explains why Evans-Pritchard's original text and argument have endured in academic study on the subject to this day.

While Evans-Pritchard is today remembered for *Witchcraft* and its contribution to the sociology of knowledge,* this field was largely nonexistent when the book was first published in 1937. World War II* swiftly intervened, during which time Evans-Pritchard served in the British army in the Sudan. The lengthy gap between the award of his PhD from fieldwork among the Azande and the publication of *Witchcraft* also ensured that by the time Evans-Pritchard returned to academia, his career had progressed rapidly. By the time *Witchcraft* was published he had already begun working among the Nuer* people seven years earlier, and his successful publications contributed to his prestigious postwar academic posts at Cambridge and Oxford. In 1970, the British social anthropologist Mary Douglas* reflected on this postwar lull: "… remember also that Evans-Pritchard is deeply modest … It is impossible to imagine him complaining that there is more in his first book than has been noticed, or that he has been misinterpreted."[2] Evans-Pritchard's achievement with *Witchcraft* would not start to resonate until a decade after its publication, when fresh perspectives in anthropology returned attention once more to the topic of witchcraft among foreign peoples.

Limitations

Witchcraft captured, at a specific point in time, the belief system of a people whose way of life was rapidly changing. The specifics of *Witchcraft* have disappeared in the subsequent century of life in the Southern Sudan, and the potency of Evans-Pritchard's argument today rests on his theoretical contribution rather than on the modern accuracy of his ethnographic findings.

Despite his sympathetic approach to the problem of primitive belief, Evans-Pritchard wrote at a time when colonial,* gender, and class power dynamics silently conditioned anthropological encounters with "other" peoples. This limited the scholar's capacity for reflexivity:* that is, the ability to reflect on the structural factors, such as class, gender, or race, that might make anthropologists see the world in a certain way, or enable their access to certain groups. Evans-Pritchard's sense of the fundamental "otherness" of primitive peoples was deeply entrenched, although he couched this in terms of respect: "One cannot really become a Zande* or a Nuer or a Bedouin* Arab," he wrote, "and the best compliment one can pay them is to remain apart from them in essentials."³

Perhaps the most glaring omissions in *Witchcraft* are the beliefs of women in Azande society, among whom we must assume Evans-Pritchard spent little time. We periodically see snippets of their lives: he describes how their exclusion from the poison oracle* forbids women from challenging the social order by asking questions about their husbands;⁴ he concludes that Azande women were "shy and tongue-tied," rather than that they might have been intimidated by the Western anthropologist.⁵ The limitations of *Witchcraft* are largely attributable to its positioning in a relatively new discipline, and immature strategies of methodological* reflection. This would have to wait until the postcolonial* era, when anthropology took a decidedly postmodern* shift (postmodernism was an academic movement in the late twentieth century, in which the certainty of scientific knowledge in the social sciences* such as anthropology and sociology was rigorously questioned and undermined).

NOTES

1 Edward Evans-Pritchard, *Witchcraft, Oracles, and Magic among the Azande* (Oxford: Clarendon Press, 1976), 16.

2 Mary Douglas, "Thirty Years after Witchcraft, Oracles and Magic," in *Witchcraft Confessions and Accusations*, ed. Mary Douglas (London: Tavistock Publications, 1970), xiv.

3 Evans-Pritchard, *Witchcraft*, 243.

4 Evans-Pritchard, *Witchcraft,* 164.

5 Evans-Pritchard, *Witchcraft,* 247.

MODULE 8
PLACE IN THE AUTHOR'S WORK

KEY POINTS

- Evans-Pritchard's anthropological* career focused on the peoples of Africa.

- *Witchcraft, Oracles, and Magic among the Azande* is an ahistorical contribution to anthropology, written in a "timeless present" tense. His later work is more historical.

- Evans-Pritchard is best known for his early work, including *Witchcraft* and his ethnography* of the Nuer* people. The fieldwork* for both books took place in the Southern Sudan.

Positioning

Witchcraft, Oracles, and Magic among the Azande was Edward Evans-Pritchard's earliest ethnographic monograph* (that is, a book-length, scholarly piece of writing). He had previously written some papers on the field of religious belief in anthropology,[1] as well as the occasional brief article reporting on short fieldwork.[2] Despite appearing relatively early in his academic career, the text demonstrated elements of Evans-Pritchard's intellectual agenda that would recur throughout his life.

Evans-Pritchard frequently changed his mind as to whether anthropology should either attempt to establish social scientific laws, or record for posterity the traditions and culture of disappearing peoples. This perhaps reflected the ongoing tension between historicity* (the belief that something factually developed as a result of certain practices in the past, rather than being a historical myth or fiction) and present-oriented functionalism* in anthropology. At the

> ❝ I did not want to become ... just an intellectual. I wanted a life of adventure too, and fieldwork seemed to be the solution to combine both. ❞
>
> Edward Evans-Pritchard, "Genesis of a Social Anthropologist: An Autobiographical Note"

time of *Witchcraft,* he later wrote, the functionalist anthropological climate was such that he might well not have bothered with extensive documentation of Azande* traditions.[3] Nonetheless, *Witchcraft* shows that Evans-Pritchard's instincts were to expand knowledge by describing disappearing ways of life.

Evans-Pritchard did not publish on the Azande again for many years. In the first edition of *Witchcraft,* he wrote, "If I have paid no particular attention to [their] history this is not because I consider it unimportant but because I consider it so important that I desire to record it in detail elsewhere."[4] This "detail" would not emerge until near the end of his life, when *The Zande Trickster* (1967) and the 444-page *The Azande: History and Political Institutions* (1971) demonstrated an explicit shift toward history and politics.

Integration

Evans-Pritchard's studies ranged from religion to magic,* kinship, social organization, and politics, united by a fascination with the rapidly changing peoples of Africa in the colonial-era* twentieth century. The social anthropologist Mary Douglas* argues that Evans-Pritchard was broadly preoccupied with the construction of a sociology of knowledge.* Commentators have noted that within his endeavor it is difficult to identify a single coherent theoretical orientation, and near the end of his life Evans-Pritchard himself forcefully wrote that "consistency is the worst of all vices in science."[5]

The anthropologist J. A. Barnes* notes that, despite his disagreements with the pioneer of functionalism Bronislaw Malinowski* and the advocate of structural-functionalism* Alfred Radcliffe-Brown,*[6] disparate passages in Evans-Pritchard's work have been used to support various types of functionalism and structural-functionalism. Structural-functionalism was the period of transition in anthropology from functionalism to structuralism in the mid-twentieth century, when the emphasis moved to the structural factors (gender, for example) that defined the function of some aspect of social or cultural life. The social scientist Meyer Fortes's* observation that Evans-Pritchard was essentially a humanist* recurs in Barnes's short biography: he was interested in people, and willing to be guided intellectually by their concerns, reflecting the humanist understanding that all human life has value and dignity.

It seems that Evans-Pritchard experimented with theoretical orientation throughout his academic career, choosing whatever helped him make sense of his primary enthusiasms: first, people; and second, adventure. The broad intellectual interests evident across his life's work demonstrate the creative resilience of an anthropologist whose early career was challenging. Yet there is no doubt that a theme unites both of his most enduring contributions: the anthropology of belief, and his reflections on the nature of anthropology itself. His early interests in the rationality of belief in Azande witchcraft,* the Nuer concept of *kwoth** (spirit), and Nuer perception of time, presented a question about the limits of anthropological "science" for the analysis of inner life.* "At this point the theologian* [that is, a person who has read and studied religious thought and ideas] takes over from the anthropologist," he wrote in the last line of *Nuer Religion* in 1956.[7] The anthropologist Matthew Engelke* has argued that for Evans-Pritchard "belief became an element of method," enabling him to comprehend the inner life of his research subjects in a manner missed by his more secular* colleagues.[8]

Significance

Today Evans-Pritchard is best known for the major works of his early career: *Witchcraft, Oracles, and Magic among the Azande* (1937), *The Nuer* (1940) and *Nuer Religion* (1956), and his coedited volume with Meyer Fortes, *African Political Systems* (1940). These early works contain the intellectual grains of much of Evans-Pritchard's theoretical contribution. He frequently changed his mind about whether anthropology should discern patterns or record fast-disappearing customs, but the content of *Witchcraft* demonstrates his lifelong intellectual desire to do both.

Witchcraft's significance in the context of his work is that it captures a particular ahistorical style in anthropology pre–World War II.* This influenced Evans-Pritchard's early intellectual attempts to position himself in anthropology after his historical training. While its subject matter might be tradition and custom, *Witchcraft* makes no mention of social or historical context. Similarly, Barnes argues, "the sparse style in which *The Nuer* is written makes it easy for the busy or lazy reader … to fall into the trap of treating the Nuer as if they lived in some timeless anthropological never-never land rather than in the Sudan of the early twentieth century."[9] Indeed, Evans-Pritchard's concerted historical turn would have to wait until the 1960s and his lecture "Anthropology and History."[10]

NOTES

1   Edward Evans-Pritchard, "The Morphology and Function of Magic: A Comparative Study of Trobriand and Zande Ritual and Spells," *American Anthropologist* 31, no. 4 (1929): 619–41; Evans-Pritchard, "The Intellectualist (English) Interpretation of Magic," *Bulletin of the Faculty of Arts* 1 (Egyptian University, Cairo, 1933): 282–311.

2   Edward Evans-Pritchard, "A Preliminary Account of the Ingassana Tribe in Fung Province," *Sudan Notes and Records* 10 (1927): 69–83.

3   Edward Evans-Pritchard, *The Azande: History and Political Institutions* (Oxford: Clarendon Press, 1971), x.

4   Edward Evans-Pritchard, *Witchcraft, Oracles, and Magic among the Azande* (Oxford: Clarendon Press, 1937), 19.

5   Edward Evans-Pritchard, "Social Anthropology at Oxford," *Man* 5, no. 4 (1970): 704.

6   J. A. Barnes, "Edward Evans-Pritchard: 1902–1973," *Proceedings of the British Academy* 73 (1987): 458.

7   Edward Evans-Pritchard, *Nuer Religion* (Oxford: Clarendon Press, 1956), 322.

8   Matthew Engelke, "The Problem of Belief: Evans-Pritchard and Victor Turner on 'The Inner Life,'" *Anthropology Today* 18, no. 6 (2002): 4.

9   Barnes, "Edward Evans-Pritchard," 464.

10 Reproduced in Edward Evans-Pritchard, *Essays in Social Anthropology* (New York: Free Press of Glencoe, 1963).

SECTION 3
IMPACT

MODULE 9
THE FIRST RESPONSES

KEY POINTS

- *Witchcraft, Oracles, and Magic among the Azande* did not immediately attract academic attention. Evans-Pritchard's former mentor Bronislaw Malinowski* was critical of early drafts of the work and attacked his methodological* integrity.

- Evans-Pritchard took this criticism personally, but maintained a lifelong interest in the construction of anthropological* writing.

- Rivalry at the London School of Economics,* where Evans-Pritchard had studied under Malinowski and gained his PhD, probably affected the early reception of the ideas in *Witchcraft*.

Criticism

In the first decade after its publication, *Witchcraft, Oracles, and Magic among the Azande* went largely unnoticed. It was Edward Evans-Pritchard's later work on the Sudanese Nuer* people—their "modes of livelihood and political institutions"—that appeared to have more of an immediate impact upon theory and research in anthropology in the postwar period. This reflected a shift of academic focus in response to World War I,* away from religious belief and toward politics. The British social anthropologist Mary Douglas* suggests that this obscured the immediate response to *Witchcraft*.

There also evidence that his one-time mentor Bronislaw Malinowski challenged Evans-Pritchard's work in *Witchcraft* and also in the shorter papers on the Azande* that had constituted his PhD at the London School of Economics.[1] Malinowski had argued that his own fieldwork* among the Trobriand Islanders* of Papua New

> ❝ One suspects that *Witchcraft, Oracles, and Magic among the Azande* is not frequently read. ❞
>
> Mary Douglas, *Edward Evans-Pritchard*

Guinea yielded general laws about the use of magic* in primitive societies. Evans-Pritchard used the example of Azande magic to disagree. He argued that a comparative rather than singular project was necessary in order to reveal such laws, and that it was too early in the comparative study of the anthropology of magic to discern them.[2] The historian of anthropology Christopher Morton* has shown that at the seminar where Evans-Pritchard presented his paper, Malinowski attacked his fieldwork methods, reportedly suggesting that he had "cooked" or "faked" his ethnographic* findings in order to produce the results he desired.[3]

While this seems to have been intended as a forthright pedagogical* challenge (that is, related to the methods and practices of teaching), it upset Evans-Pritchard profoundly. He struggled to find a permanent job for some years after his PhD was awarded, and apparently attributed this to falling out with his distinguished former mentor.[4] Coincidentally, after *Witchcraft*'s publication and as World War II* broke out, Malinowski left Britain for a position at Yale University* in the United States, so it is not known how the older anthropologist responded to the final published version of Evans-Pritchard's work among the Azande.

Responses

The most substantial criticisms of the ideas in *Witchcraft* have arisen following various paradigm shifts in anthropology—fundamental changes in the field's basic assumptions and methods—in the years since Evans-Pritchard's death in 1973. Nonetheless, we can gather some sense of how Evans-Pritchard responded to criticism in his own lifetime, both from Christopher Morton's notes and from J. A. Barnes's* insightful memoir. As a young anthropologist, Evans-Pritchard had responded with hurt feelings and insecurity to Malinowski's dig at his credibility as a social scientist. On that occasion he allowed himself to be guided by his supervisor Charles Seligman* and wrote a contrite and endearingly intellectual apology, reflecting on the methodological difficulty of constructing argument from fact. This enduring preoccupation is discernable in Appendix IV of the 1976 *Witchcraft* edition, in which Evans-Pritchard reflects, "the decisive battle is not fought in the field but in the study afterward … The theoretical conclusions will then be found to be implicit in an exact and detailed description."[5]

Throughout his academic career, Evans-Pritchard participated earnestly in debates about the methodology of anthropological writing, which made him consider superficial critiques of his own work to be all the more irritating. Later in his life, when he was a successful professor of anthropology at Oxford, he was equally "exasperated by critics who appeared to have read only one item of his writings, or who had taken a passage out of context." However he loved to engage with students who had read his work carefully and came to the debate armed with their own field observations.[6]

Conflict and Consensus

Christopher Morton reports that Evans-Pritchard's relationship with Malinowski entered a new phase after the younger anthropologist's appointment to the University of Cairo* in 1932—possibly thanks to geographical distance. Connecticut College professor of anthropology John Burton* comments that even while Evans-Pritchard "claimed to have loathed the man in public settings, it is evident that the quality and breadth of his ethnographic contributions were in a significant way the direct manifestation of Malinowski's inspiration upon his thought."[7] Indeed, throughout Evans-Pritchard's work he notably—

and with equal vehemence—critiques and praises his various intellectual patrons. Tantalizingly, Malinowski's death in 1942, mid-World War II, meant that we will never know whether the two might have forged a more fertile and consensus-based critical relationship after the publication of *Witchcraft*.

Moreover, the themes of contention shifted dramatically post-World War II. Malinowski's critiques of the young anthropologist had largely concerned method and ethnographic writing. Christopher Morton argues that this was symptomatic of a pedagogical climate of competition and rivalry at the London School of Economics, as anthropologists fought to establish precedence in the rapidly changing field. By the time *Witchcraft* once again seized attention in anthropology, Evans-Pritchard was an established academic at the University of Oxford. New critiques of the text had emerged from the critical distance made possible by the passing of decades.

NOTES

1   Jack Goody, *The Expansive Moment: The Rise of Social Anthropology in Britain and Africa 1918–1970* (Cambridge: Cambridge University Press 1995).

2   Edward Evans-Pritchard, "The Morphology and Function of Magic: A Comparative Study of Trobriand and Zande Ritual and Spells," *American Anthropologist* 31, no. 4 (1929): 619–41.

3   Christopher Morton, "Evans-Pritchard and Malinowski: The Roots of a Complex Relationship," *History of Anthropology Newsletter* 34, no. 2 (2007): 10–14.

4   Morton, "Evans-Pritchard," 10–14.

5   Edward Evans-Pritchard, *Witchcraft, Oracles, and Magic among the Azande* (Oxford: Clarendon Press, 1976), 243.

6   J. A. Barnes, "Edward Evans-Pritchard: 1902–1973," *Proceedings of the British Academy*, 73 (1987): 481.

7   John Burton, "The Ghost of Malinowski in the Southern Sudan: Evans-Pritchard and Ethnographic Fieldwork," *Proceedings of the American Philosophical Society* 127, no. 4 (1983): 279.

THE EVOLVING DEBATE

KEY POINTS

- After the publication of *Witchcraft* in 1937, the key reading of the text's ideas was that witchcraft* was about struggles for power within suffering societies.

- The study of witchcraft flourished in the disciplines of history and philosophy, and anthropology* began to investigate witchcraft beliefs in "modern" societies.

- Anthropology now studies both the problems of "inner life"* as well as social context.

Uses and Problems

The British social anthropologist Mary Douglas* was sanguine about the initial legacy of Edward Evans-Pritchard's *Witchcraft, Oracles, and Magic among the Azande*: "[*Witchcraft*] might have been expected to stimulate more studies on the social restraints upon perception. Instead it fathered studies of micro-politics. The relation between belief and society, instead of appearing as infinitely complex, subtle, and fluid, was presented as a control system with negative feedback."[1]

These ideas were moved forward in the 1950s and 1960s by anthropologists such as Victor Turner,* J. Clyde Mitchell,* and M. G. Marwick* of the Manchester School*—the school of thought developed by the department of anthropology at the University of Manchester. They advanced the ideas by portraying witchcraft accusations as the result of cyclical struggles for power within oversized settlements.[2] This paved the way for an anthropological backlash against notions of witchcraft as a constructive force. Indeed, the German anthropologist Philip Mayer* argued that witchcraft

> **❝** The excitement the book provoked was palpable even in the 1980s. **❞**
>
> Tanya Luhrmann, "What Anthropology Should Learn from G. E. R. Lloyd"

accusations were symptoms of a "sick society" and that witchcraft beliefs were harmful.[3]

An interest in dynamism and complexity returned to investigations of witchcraft in the 1980s and 1990s. The Dutch anthropologist Peter Geschiere* sought to build upon Evans-Pritchard's participant-observation.* He wanted to better understand the role played by witchcraft belief in expressing disrupted social life and structure. The anthropologist must "venture into more vague spheres and try to make sense of the turmoil of rumors," argued Geschiere.[4]

More recently, however, critics have questioned the extent to which witchcraft beliefs can be seen as symbolic representations of unfortunate events and societal changes. The anthropologist Harry West* of the School of Oriental and African Studies in London argues that witchcraft beliefs are not merely metaphorical, but involve people acting on the invisible realm with the intention of having very real effects on the material world.[5]

Schools of Thought

Witchcraft has influenced the anthropology of witchcraft, religion, and belief. A key contribution was to collapse the pejorative distinction between "primitive" and "modern" modes of thought. Academics began to study cultures across the globe—not just the "primitive"— and the relationship between witchcraft beliefs and social change. In the 1990s, Geschiere argued that witchcraft beliefs and accusations have actually increased with the rise of "modernity" and globalization.* In the past 40 years, Birgit Meyer* and Peter Pels,* Jeanne Favret-Saada,* and Tanya Luhrmann* have all persuasively described the existence of witchcraft and magic* in "modern" societies.[6]

Evans-Pritchard's early interdisciplinary* training enabled broad academic take-up of his ideas. Distinctive strands of British anthropology are now concerned with history, and the philosophy and epistemology* (study of knowledge) of science. The historian Alan Macfarlane* trained in anthropology, and with fellow historian Keith Thomas* transformed the study of witchcraft and popular religion in early-modern Britain.[7] The sociologist* Struan Jacobs* argues that Evans-Pritchard's topic of discrepancies or "logical gaps" in belief systems was influential in philosophy to an extent that has not been recognized.[8] Philosopher Michael Polanyi* was struck by the "fiduciary element" of knowledge: the way that "trust" fills gaps and undermines internal contradictions in both "scientific" and "religious" knowledge. Polanyi then influenced others in the philosophy of science.[9]

In Current Scholarship

Today it is rare that an ethnography* about witchcraft or magic in Africa does not refer to Evans-Pritchard's work in *Witchcraft*. Yet its influence is diffused; the changing landscape of the discipline means that there is no longer a distinct school of thought allied to Evans-Pritchard that could be attributed to *Witchcraft*. Eighty years in anthropology have enabled the integration of ideas from history, philosophy, and psychology. These have changed the intellectual climate in which the science of social and cultural life is attempted.

Nevertheless, Evans-Pritchard's interests are alive in anthropology today. His intention to contribute to the anthropology of knowledge* has come full circle in the past 30 years with anthropology's renewed interest in epistemology. For example, the anthropologists Tanya Luhrmann and Annemarie Mol,* both working in Western cultures, seek to understand how beliefs arise and are used.[10] They analyze how mutually contradictory beliefs are reconciled in contexts where they come into close contact, and therefore how individuals participate in maintaining the integrity of belief systems. Evans-Pritchard's legacy also continues at the University of Oxford—its establishment of "medical anthropology"* as a separate program in the past 15 years is testimony to its figurehead's formative interest in the remedy of misfortune across cultures. Meanwhile, the anthropologies of ritual and morality are vibrant areas of research among scholars around the world.

NOTES

1   Mary Douglas, "Thirty Years after Witchcraft, Oracles and Magic," in *Witchcraft Confessions and Accusations*, ed. Mary Douglas (London: Tavistock Publications, 1970), xiv.

2   Victor Turner, *Schism and Continuity in an African Society: A Study of Ndembu Village Life* (Manchester: Manchester University Press for Rhodes Livingstone Institute, 1957); J. Clyde Mitchell, *The Yao Village: A Study in the Social Structure of a Nyasaland Tribe* (Manchester: Manchester University Press for Rhodes Livingstone Institute, 1956); M. G. Marwick, *Sorcery in its Social Setting: A Study of the Northern Rhodesian Cewa* (Manchester: Manchester University Press, 1965).

3   P. Mayer, "Witches" (Inaugural Lecture, Rhodes University, Grahamstown, 1954).

4   Peter Geschiere, *The Modernity of Witchcraft: Politics and the Occult in Postcolonial Africa* (Charlottesville: University Press of Virginia, 1997), 219.

5   Harry West, *Kupilikula: Governance and the Invisible Realm in Mozambique* (Chicago: University of Chicago Press, 2005).

6   Birgit Meyer and Peter Pels, eds., *Magic and Modernity: Interfaces of Revelation and Concealment* (Stanford: Stanford University Press, 2003).

7   Alan Macfarlane, *Witchcraft in Tudor and Stuart England: A Regional and Comparative Study* (London: Routledge and Kegan Paul, 1970).

8   Struan Jacobs, "Two sources of Michael Polanyi's Prototypal Notion of Incommensurability: Evans-Pritchard on Azande Witchcraft and St. Augustine on Conversion," *History of the Human Sciences* 16, no. 2 (2003): 57–76.

9   Michael Polanyi, *Personal Knowledge: Towards a Post-Critical Philosophy* (London: Routledge & Kegan Paul, 1958), 287–94.

10 Tanya Luhrmann, *Of Two Minds: The Growing Disorder in American Psychiatry* (London: Picador, 2000); Annemarie Mol, *The Body Multiple: Ontology in Medical Practice* (Durham, North Carolina: Duke University Press, 2002).

IMPACT AND INFLUENCE TODAY

KEY POINTS

- Today *Witchcraft, Oracles, and Magic among the Azande* is a classic text in the anthropology* of witchcraft.*

- The ideas in *Witchcraft* still challenge those considering the appropriate methods for the anthropological study of belief and "inner life."*

- Anthropologists now argue that their increased participation in belief systems produces better findings.

Position

Today, *Witchcraft, Oracles, and Magic among the Azande* is understood to be the key originator of the anthropological study of witchcraft. While Edward Evans-Pritchard's work is much less frequently discussed in contemporary anthropology than it was from the 1950s to the 1980s, *Witchcraft* retains an implicit importance in the ideas and practices of anthropologists. Today, anthropological studies across the globe take as their basic point of departure the fact that varying social, political, and environmental contexts fundamentally generate different world views and experiences of perception; and anthropologists take as their basic point of method that they must participate in the cultures they claim to observe.

Witchcraft's classical exemplification of early anthropology, its famously clear writing and rich ethnographic* detail explain its endurance as a staple of undergraduate reading lists. It invites reflection upon the development of anthropological methods, fieldwork* ethics, and theoretical orientations, as well as upon its intellectual subjects: belief, perception, witchcraft, magic,* and cultural systems.

> 66 Now that the air has cleared and now that philosophers have worked through the pitfalls of earlier controversies, Evans-Pritchard emerges from the past as if he had, impossibly, been reared in a modern theory of knowledge ... he was legitimately ahead of the game. 99
>
> Mary Douglas, *Edward Evans-Pritchard*

Anthropological understandings of these latter subjects have moved on. Yet the personal nature of anthropological method means that much is still to be gained from inquiry into the ethics of Evans-Pritchard's use of a Zande* servant as informant*[1] or his deliberate disruption of Azande* ritual.[2] These points of controversy have given Evans-Pritchard a methodological* as well as an intellectual legacy in anthropology.

Interaction
Evans-Pritchard argued that witchcraft perceptions and beliefs were highly context-specific, and that although one could partially participate in these, one could never truly "become" a Zande or a Nuer.*[3] With the rise of postmodernism* in the later twentieth century, a philosophical approach that challenges the security of definitions and the idea of objective truth altogether, this ethical and methodological issue inspired and challenged the anthropologists who studied witchcraft in Western societies.

The anthropology of "belief" and knowledge became crucial to the ongoing debate over whether one should "participate" or "observe" as an anthropologist. Jeanne Favret-Saada's* important study of witchcraft in 1970s France controversially demonstrated the extent of anthropological participation required in order to access the "inner life" of witchcraft: she explained to the colleagues who had attempted to suppress her publication, "one cannot study witchcraft without agreeing to take part in the situations where it manifests itself, and in the discourse expressing it."[4] Her highly involved level of participation, of which perhaps Evans-Pritchard would have disapproved, nonetheless paid homage to his own emphasis on the contextual specificity of how beliefs are expressed.

Tanya Luhrmann's* work, meanwhile, shows a turn in the anthropology of knowledge* toward deconstruction of "belief." She favors instead an attitude of pragmatism; for her, "beliefs are not the sorts of things they are stereotypically assumed to be: propositional commitments held consciously and claimed consistently and in a logical relationship to other such commitments." Beliefs, rather, "do a job; they are not always disinterestedly asserted because they are felt to be true in themselves."[5] This would arguably have been a very compatible position for Evans-Pritchard. It raised both the issues of the "job" of maintaining social and moral order, and the maneuvering capacity of the individuals who had to do it.

The Continuing Debate

If the enactment and expression of "beliefs" are pragmatic and context-specific, *Witchcraft* continues to challenge anthropologists who question the "reality" of different belief systems and the conscious intention of those who enact them. Evans-Pritchard was clear: Azande beliefs were rational, but based on false premises. Witches did not exist; nor were witchcraft, oracles,* or magic real in the sense that they tangibly existed outside the minds of his informants. While many in contemporary anthropology broadly agree, others suggest that the materiality* of Western scientific assumptions hobbles our analysis of belief ("materiality" is an emphasis on the importance of material factors).

The anthropologist Harry West* argues that supernatural beliefs cannot be assumed to be merely metaphors for more "concrete" phenomena and experiences. For the believers, the existence of spiritual forces and beings is just as "real" as the existence of those inhabiting the material realm.[6]

To clarify appropriate anthropological method in this area, the anthropologist Paul Stoller* advocated the "suspension of disbelief": that the anthropologist considers the foreign belief system to have the fuzziness of possibility, rather than determining it to be either definite or impossible.[7] By contrast, more recently, the anthropologist Matthew Engelke* has argued that despite Evans–Pritchard's refutation of the reality of Azande spiritual and religious beliefs, his own "religious conviction became a tool in [his] anthropological projects, a way of bridging the distance between [himself] and 'the other.'"[8] Opinion among contemporary anthropologists remains divided on whether one's own religious belief might be a help or hindrance.

NOTES

1   Edward Evans-Pritchard, *Witchcraft, Oracles, and Magic among the Azande* (Oxford: Clarendon Press, 1976), 102.

2   Evans-Pritchard, *Witchcraft*, 103.

3   Evans-Pritchard, *Witchcraft*, 243.

4   Jeanne Favret-Saada, *Deadly Words: Witchcraft in the Bocage* (Cambridge: Cambridge University Press, 1980), 20.

5   Tanya Luhrmann, *Persuasions of the Witch's Craft: Ritual Magic and Witchcraft in Present-Day England* (Oxford: Basil Blackwell, 1989), 384.

6   Harry West, *Ethnographic Sorcery* (Chicago: University of Chicago Press, 2008).

7   Paul Stoller, *Fusion of the Worlds: An Ethnography of Possession Among the Songhay of Niger* (Chicago: University of Chicago Press, 1989).

8   Matthew Engelke, "The Problem of Belief: Evans-Pritchard and Victor Turner on 'The Inner Life,'" *Anthropology Today* 18, no. 6 (2002): 8.

WHERE NEXT?

KEY POINTS

- *Witchcraft, Oracles, and Magic among the Azande* will likely
  be reread in the light of the ongoing dialogue between
  anthropology's* reflection on itself, and its customary
  analysis of "other" peoples.

- Theoretical developments in the anthropology of
  knowledge,* ritual, and personhood* (that is, the way
  individuals intersect with the requirements of their society)
  ensure Evans-Pritchard's interests survive.

- *Witchcraft* remains seminal because of its humanist*
  contribution to the topic of belief in non-Western societies.
  Humanism is a strand of ethical thought attributing the
  most value and dignity to human life.

Potential

Edward Evans-Pritchard's *Witchcraft, Oracles, and Magic among the
Azande* continues to be a point of reference in debates about the
nature of reality and construction of knowledge: "Perspectivism* and
multiple ontologies* have become, I think, the new Azande," writes
Tanya Luhrmann.[1] Perspectivism is a term coined to describe an
Amazonian philosophy comparable with cultural relativism,* the
view that values are best understood within their own cultural context.
The term "multiple ontologies" is the idea that there are many ways to
experience reality, each equally "real" to the participants.

Despite attracting accusations of narcissism, the later twentieth-
century swing toward the philosophical approach of postmodernism,*
with its challenge to the security of the idea of "objective truth," and
reflexivity* provided a necessary counterpart to the authoritative

> 66 This is an immensely exciting moment for anthropology in general. It suggests that we are past self-recriminations and self-absorption and that we are getting on with the business of making sense of other people. 99
>
> Tanya Luhrmann, "What Anthropology Should Learn from G. E. R. Lloyd"

anthropology of Evans-Pritchard's era. Anthropology in the twenty-first century has the chance to integrate the self-reflective insights of postmodernism with anthropology's earliest intellectual agenda of understanding others. The topics offered by *Witchcraft* are sufficiently timeless that such projects remain open-ended.

Potential inspiration for these future endeavors is diverse. As anthropologists seek to understand the lived experience of ritual and the pragmatic navigation of illness and misfortune, phenomenology* (the study of the structures of consciousness and experience) has enjoyed a comeback in medical anthropology.* The new anthropologies of ethics (roughly, "right behavior") and morality continue the research toward a better understanding of how and why we participate in the maintenance and development of the moral order. Anthropologists continue to develop theories about the never-ending interaction between the individual and society, and the collective construction of meaning. Increased scholarly interest in *Witchcraft's* 1937 edition and its emphasis on the ordinary nature of witchcraft* has the potential to revitalize the anthropology of personhood, intention, and agency* (a person's capacity to behave effectively under certain conditions).

Future Directions
Several established anthropologists are obvious candidates to continue the development of these intellectual agendas. Tanya Luhrmann has

worked on witchcraft in London, personhood in American psychiatry, and evangelical Christianity in the United States.[2] Her ethnographies* combine a desire to capture the context-specific experience of beliefs, assumptions, and actions with big-picture analysis that yields broader insights into the social and cultural contexts of belief. Thomas Csordas* has had a fruitful academic career investigating the embodied experience of Catholic Charismatic* ritual healing in the United States and recently surveyed literature on witchcraft as a means to reopen interest in the anthropology of morality.[3] "Catholic Charismatic" refers to a spiritual movement in the Roman Catholic Church in the United States that emphasizes a personal relationship with Jesus, and faith healing.

The anthropology of knowledge and perception remains vibrant in the Institute of Social and Cultural Anthropology at Oxford University, an institution associated with Evans-Pritchard, where Elisabeth Hsu* works on the epistemology* of healing in China.[4] Meanwhile, problems of intentionality and morality have been newly reinvigorated by Keith M. Murphy* and C. Jason Throop* and colleagues, working in contexts across the globe in which concepts of health and belief interact.[5] Martin Mills* of the University of Aberdeen has recently undertaken further analysis of the relationships among personhood, belief, and agency, based upon his critical rereading of *Witchcraft* in its 1937 edition.[6] Now, nearly 80 years after its first publication, *Witchcraft* will doubtless prove inspirational for anthropologists for many years to come.

Summary

Edward Evans-Pritchard's *Witchcraft, Oracles, and Magic among the Azande* ranks as a classic text in social anthropology. It established research agendas that endure in the discipline, despite changing theoretical orientations. Evans-Pritchard trained at a time of pioneering development in anthropology in Britain—when a young man with good connections, a thirst for adventure, and a certain amount of intellectual curiosity could make a tangible contribution. From the subject of religious belief, to witchcraft, perception, and social organization in small-scale societies, Evans-Pritchard bound together topics of universal intellectual appeal in a specific study of one small, thoroughly non-European, and fast-changing group in the Southern Sudan.

In today's increasingly globalized* world (one of increasing political, cultural, and economic ties across continental boundaries), *Witchcraft* captures an African society before it changed beyond recognition because of a different kind of connection: colonialism.* Today it is read as much for its silences—what it does not say—as for what it does. Evans-Pritchard was one of the first anthropologists to steer the discipline away from the essentializing split between "us" and "them" that was evident in the work of his forebears in anthropology and philosophy, and that had emerged out of the colonialism of the eighteenth and nineteenth centuries. Instead he attempted to open up the analysis of "mentality" to a more culturally relativist position, in which the beliefs of the Azande* were understood on their own terms. His conclusions that Azande belief was logical and coherent were all the more radical, and continue to position *Witchcraft* as an innovative text in the history of anthropology.

NOTES

1 Tanya Luhrmann, "What Anthropology Should Learn from G. E. R. Lloyd," *Journal of Ethnographic Theory* 3, no. 1 (2013): 171–3.

2 Tanya Luhrmann, *Persuasions of the Witch's Craft: Ritual Magic and Witchcraft in Present-Day England* (Oxford: Basil Blackwell, 1989); Luhrmann, *Of Two Minds: The Growing Division in American Psychiatry* (London: Picador, 2000); Luhrmann, *When God Talks Back: Understanding the American Evangelical Relationship with God* (New York: Albert Knopf, 2012).

3   Thomas Csordas, *The Sacred Self* (Berkeley: University of California Press, 1994); Csordas, "Morality as a Cultural System," *Current Anthropology* 54, no. 5 (2013): 523–46.

4   Elisabeth Hsu, *The Transmission of Chinese Medicine* (Cambridge: Cambridge University Press, 1999).

5   Keith M. Murphy and C. Jason Throop, *Toward an Anthropology of the Will* (Stanford: Stanford University Press, 2010).

6   Martin Mills, "The Opposite of Witchcraft: Evans-Pritchard and the Problem of the Person," *Journal of the Royal Anthropological Institute* 19 (2013): 18–33.

GLOSSARY

GLOSSARY OF TERMS

Agency: the capacity of individuals to act effectively under certain conditions.

Anglicanism: a Protestant tradition within Christianity, dating back to the Reformation (the split between the Protestant and older Catholic branches of Christianity) and comprising the Church of England and allied churches.

Animism: the belief that non-human things or beings, such as rocks, trees, or animals, have spiritual properties.

Anthropology: the qualitative or quantitative study of human social and cultural life, including domains "at home" as well as those of distant countries.

Anthropology of knowledge: the qualitative study of human social and cultural variation in belief, perception, intention, and the transmission of knowledge.

Autopsy: a surgical procedure that the Azande conducted following the death of a person suspected of being a witch, to determine whether the intestines contained "witchcraft-substance," and therefore whether the person was indeed a witch.

Avongara: the "aristocracy", or elite members of the Azande people.

Azande: the small-scale agriculturalist people living in the Southern Sudan, among whom Evans-Pritchard conducted fieldwork.

Bedouin: an Arabian semi-nomadic people who have historically lived in the deserts of the Middle East.

Catholic Charismatic Renewal: a spiritual movement in the Catholic Church in the United States, which emphasizes a personal relationship with Jesus, and the "expression" of the gifts of the Holy Spirit through faith healing.

Collective representations: a term coined by the pioneering French sociologist Émile Durkheim to describe a symbol that has collective meaning to the members of a particular society.

Colonialism: the practice of invading, occupying, and controlling foreign lands and peoples.

Cosmology: the perspective in philosophy that inquires into the general (and cross-cultural) laws of the universe, including its properties of time and space.

Cultural relativism: the perspective that norms and values are best understood within their specific cultural context.

Enlightenment: a philosophical and political movement in the eighteenth century that celebrated the power of rationality and the importance of liberty and the individual.

Epistemology: the study of knowledge, including belief, perception, intention, and the transmission of knowledge.

Ethnography: the written text containing the findings and analysis of anthropological study; the practice of recording and collating such findings.

Evolutionism: in regard to culture, the idea that cultures evolve in one direction, from primitivism to scientific modernity.

Fieldwork: in regard to anthropology, the practice of conducting social scientific investigation among human societies, usually for extended periods of time.

Functionalism: in regard to anthropology, the idea that all aspects of social life exist to maintain the survival and coherence of the social order.

Globalization: the process of connection through the increased international circulation of ideas, products, and persons.

Granary: among the Azande, a storehouse for grain, on stilts with a shaded area underneath.

Hamlet: the central character, philosophical and inquiring by nature, in the play of the same name by William Shakespeare.

Hereditary: transmitted by inheritance; among the Azande, witchcraft passed from father to son.

Historicity: the idea that something factually originated and developed through specific human practices in the past, rather than being a universal, unchanging phenomenon.

Humanism: a strand of ethical thought in modern social sciences attributing paramount value and dignity to human life.

Hunter–gatherer society: one in which food is obtained by gathering wild plants or hunting animals, rather than by planned agriculture or animal husbandry.

Hypothesis: an explanation for a phenomenon made on the basis of the available evidence, or in anticipation of discovering particular evidence.

Informant: in regard to anthropology, a person who is a key source of information for the researcher about the social or cultural practices and ideas of a group.

Inner life: a term sometimes used in anthropology to describe experience, perception, and belief. Although these are "inner," and therefore "hidden," and the subject of psychology, they are also key subjects in anthropology.

Interdisciplinary: bringing together more than one field of academic study.

Kwoth: the Nuer term for "spirit," also sometimes translated as "God."

London School of Economics: a prestigious social and political science research university in London, where early British anthropology flourished.

Magic: the use of substances, language, and action to effect change via supernatural forces; among the Azande, magic was used to harm witches in revenge.

Manchester School: the department of anthropology at the University of Manchester, founded by Max Gluckman in 1947, and particularly interested in conflict in small-scale societies.

Materiality: in regard to anthropology, the quality of being made up of physical substance or matter.

Medical anthropology: the qualitative or quantitative study of medical or health-related domains of social and cultural life, from shamans to psychiatrists.

Methodology: the system and analysis of methods through which anthropologists gather qualitative or quantitative data about their topic of study.

Missionary: a member of an evangelical religious group (usually Christian), working abroad to encourage conversion to their religion.

Monograph: in regard to anthropology, a book-length academic work.

Multiple ontologies: in regard to anthropology, the idea that there are multiple ways of experiencing reality, each equally "real" to their respective participants.

Mysticism: belief in experiences that transcend physical reality.

Nuer: the pastoral (livestock-subsistence) people living in the Southern Sudan, among whom Evans-Pritchard conducted fieldwork in the 1930s.

Oracle: the impartial ritual authority from which the Azande could seek answers, particularly about the identity of witches. Azande oracles included the poison oracle and the rubbing board oracle; the poison oracle was regarded as the most reliable of the two.

Participant-observation: the anthropological method of spending extended periods of time participating in the social and cultural lives of other peoples, in order to better understand, describe, and analyze them scientifically.

Pathology: a suffering or deviation from the healthy norm.

Pedagogy: the methods, activities, and practices of teaching.

Personhood: the ways in which individuals intersect with the requirements and opportunities of their society, whether through social roles, obligations, or entitlements.

Perspectivism: a term coined by anthropologist Eduardo Viveiros de Castro to describe an Amazonian philosophy that is comparable with but different from cultural relativism.

Phenomenology: in regard to philosophy, the study of the structures and phenomena of consciousness and experience.

Poison oracle: the oracle that is consulted by acquiring chickens and feeding them poison in turn, asking aloud whether this man or that man is to blame for one's misfortune. If the man named is the witch, the chicken will die; if not, the chicken will recover. The injured party continues the inquiry until a named person is implicated.

Postcolonialism: the study of the legacy of Western colonialism in the nineteenth and twentieth centuries.

Postmodernism: a movement in academia in the 1980s and 1990s, in which the certainty of scientific knowledge in the humanities and social sciences was rigorously questioned and undermined.

Rationalism: a movement in philosophy in the seventeenth century, which believed that reason and rationality were the best source of knowledge.

Reflexivity: in regard to anthropology, the practice of taking into account the individual and social factors (such as class, gender, or race) that may affect the anthropologist's personal capacity to uncover social and cultural findings in the analysis of a given society.

Secularism: the viewpoint that the state and other political institutions and practices should be kept separate from religious institutions and practices.

Social science: the study of human society and relationships within that society.

Sociology of knowledge: the study (usually quantitative) of the interaction between patterns of social behavior, practices, organizations, and institutions, and the construction and transmission of knowledge.

Structural-functionalism: a term sometimes used to describe the transition in mid-twentieth-century anthropology from functionalism to structuralism, during which the emphasis shifted to the structural factors that defined the function of any given aspect of social or cultural life.

Termite: small insect that lives on dead plant material. Among the Azande, the termite oracle was a way of questioning which path a person should follow, by inserting two separate plant branches or "paths" into a termite mound and seeing which had been eaten or "chosen" by the termites the following morning.

Theism: the belief in the existence of (at least) one God.

Theology: the study of concepts of "God" and other religious ideas.

Trobriand Islands: a group of coral islands off the east coast of New Guinea, where Edward Evans-Pritchard's mentor, Bronislaw Malinowski, conducted fieldwork in the early twentieth century.

University of Cairo: known as the Egyptian University when Edward Evans-Pritchard held one of its academic posts, this is currently one of the largest institutions of higher education in the world.

Yale University: a prestigious private university in New Haven, Connecticut, United States, where Bronislaw Malinowski took up a post a few years before his death in 1942.

Witch: among the Azande, a person (usually of bad character) who intentionally or unintentionally sends witchcraft-substance to harm someone against whom a grudge is held.

Witchcraft: in Azande society, the inherited capacity to do intentional harm to another person by supernatural means.

Witch doctor: in Azande society, a person who sold magic and medicines to others, and performed rituals to help combat witchcraft.

Witchcraft-substance: in Azande society, the substance found in the intestines proving that a person was a witch, and visible in action as a bright light moving through space. It was thought to be hereditary, so its discovery in the body of a man implied that his sons and father were also witches.

World War I: a global conflict from 1914 to 1918, triggered by the assassination of Archduke Franz Ferdinand in Sarajevo, Bosnia, and including considerable land, air, and sea fighting in Europe.

World War II: a global conflict from 1939 to 1945, triggered by Adolf Hitler's invasion of Poland, and including the Holocaust of European Jews and the detonation of nuclear weapons in Japan.

Zande: the singular of "Azande," used to describe individual Azande members.

Zandeland: the region of the Southern Sudan occupied by the Azande people.

PEOPLE MENTIONED IN THE TEXT

Robert Ackerman (b. 1935) is a British historian of anthropology. His books include *J. G. Frazer: His Life and Work* (1990).

Talal Asad (b. 1932) is an anthropologist at the City University of New York, and a former student of Edward Evans-Pritchard. He has made significant contributions to the anthropology of religion and secularism.

Alan Barnard (b. 1949) is professor of anthropology at the University of Edinburgh. He specializes in the anthropology of southern Africa and the history of anthropology.

J. A. Barnes (1918–2010) was an Australian and British anthropologist at the University of Cambridge. He contributed particularly to the study of social networks.

Frederick Bartlett (1886–1969) was a British experimental psychologist at the University of Cambridge. His arguments about the selective properties of memory influenced Evans-Pritchard's hypothesis that the selective articulation of belief among the Azande helped maintain the integrity of their belief system.

John Burton (1952–2013) was a professor of anthropology and director of African Studies at Connecticut College. He is particularly known for his work on the Nilotic peoples of Eastern Africa and for his interest in Edward Evans-Pritchard's work.

Thomas Csordas (b. 1952) is a professor of anthropology and religion at the University of California, San Diego. He has predominantly researched the embodied experience of ritual healing among Catholic Charismatics in the Southern United States.

Mary Douglas (1921–2007) was a British social anthropologist renowned for her work on structure and symbolism. She was Edward Evans-Pritchard's doctoral student and a key figure in anthropology at University College London.

Émile Durkheim (1858–1917) was a French sociologist active in the late nineteenth and early twentieth centuries. He is credited with having founded French anthropology and sociology, and was a key influence for Evans-Pritchard.

Matthew Engelke (b. 1972) is a professor of anthropology at the London School of Economics. His work focuses particularly on religion, secularism, and culture in Africa and Britain.

Jeanne Favret-Saada (b. 1934) is a French anthropologist who has studied witchcraft, psychoanalysis, and blasphemy controversies. Her work on witchcraft in France in the 1970s was a key contribution to the anthropology of witchcraft in Western societies.

Meyer Fortes (1906–83) was a British social anthropologist who specialized in the political anthropology of West African peoples. He was a peer and friend of Evans-Pritchard at the London School of Economics.

James Frazer (1854–1941) was a social anthropologist, classicist, and Fellow of Trinity College, Cambridge. He is best known for his six-volume work *The Golden Bough* (1890), a comparative analysis of "primitive" religion and belief, and classical mythology.

Ernest Gellner (1925–95) was a renowned British philosopher and anthropologist. He was particularly known for his contribution to the study of nationalism.

Peter Geschiere (b. 1941) is professor of anthropology at the University of Amsterdam. His work focuses particularly on witchcraft, politics, and citizenship, in Africa and elsewhere.

Eva Gillies (1930–2011) was an interpreter and translator who studied anthropology at Oxford in the 1960s. She conducted fieldwork in Nigeria and abridged Edward Evans-Pritchard's *Witchcraft, Oracles, and Magic among the Azande* for its popular 1976 edition.

Jack Goody (1919–2015) was a renowned British social anthropologist who conducted extensive fieldwork in northern Ghana. He published widely on inheritance systems, literacy, and cognition.

Elisabeth Hsu is a professor of anthropology at the University of Oxford. Her research includes the epistemology of healing in Chinese culture, society, and history.

Struan Jacobs is a senior lecturer in sociology at Deakin University. His work focuses on social studies of science, and the intellectual history of science and social science.

Kamanga was a member of the Azande elite, and Edward Evans-Pritchard's personal servant during his fieldwork among the Azande in the 1920s. He trained as a witch doctor and became a key informant for Evans-Pritchard regarding Zande customs and beliefs.

Lucien Lévy-Bruhl (1857–1939) was a French philosopher of the late nineteenth and early twentieth centuries. Much of *Witchcraft, Oracles, and Magic among the Azande* is grounded in Evans-Pritchard's desire to refute his notion that there is a separate form of "primitive thought" that is less well developed than the thought of more "civilized" people.

Tanya Luhrmann (b. 1959) is a professor of anthropology at Stanford University. Since the 1980s she has studied belief in religious and medical domains in Western culture, investigating witchcraft in London, and the belief systems of American psychiatric training.

Alan Macfarlane (b. 1941) is an anthropologist and historian, and professor emeritus of King's College, Cambridge. He has published widely on witchcraft and religion, kinship and inheritance; his geographical focus has ranged from England to Nepal, Japan, and China.

Bronislaw Malinowski (1884–1942) was a Polish-born British social anthropologist who spent much of his career at the London School of Economics, pioneering the practice of anthropological fieldwork. He conducted several years of fieldwork among the Trobriand Islanders of Papua New Guinea (1914–18), and was considered the major figure in British anthropology in the first half of the twentieth century, publishing the highly influential *Argonauts of the Western Pacific* in 1922.

M. G. Marwick was an anthropologist at the University of Stirling who trained at the Manchester School. He published on sorcery and witchcraft in southern Africa.

Philip Mayer (1910–95) was a German anthropologist. He arrived in Britain in 1939 and received a DPhil in anthropology from the University of Oxford. He conducted research throughout Africa on witchcraft and sorcery.

Birgit Meyer (b. 1960) is professor of religious studies at Utrecht University. She specializes in West Africa and the anthropology of religion, media, and material culture.

Martin Mills is a senior lecturer in anthropology at the University of Aberdeen. His work particularly focuses on religion, personhood, and authority among Tibetan communities, and he has conducted fieldwork in Tibet, Northern India, Ladakh, and Scotland.

J. Clyde Mitchell (1918–95) was a British anthropologist and sociologist. He was a member of the Manchester School and conducted research on social systems and networks in Central Africa.

Annemarie Mol (b. 1958) is a Dutch anthropologist and philosopher at the University of Amsterdam. Her work focuses on the anthropology of the body, illness, and biomedical practice.

Christopher Morton is a lecturer in visual and material anthropology at the University of Oxford, and curator of photograph and manuscript collections at the Pitt Rivers Museum. His work focuses on the relationship between photography and anthropology, in the history of anthropology as well as the present.

Keith M. Murphy is associate professor of anthropology at the University of California at Irvine. His work focuses on language, material culture, and the nature of human experience.

Peter Pels (b. 1958) is professor in the anthropology of Africa at the University of Leiden. His research focuses on religion and politics, the anthropology of magic, and social science ethics.

Michael Polanyi (1891–1976) was a Hungarian-born philosopher and chemist who was professor of social sciences at the University of Manchester. He argued in *Personal Knowledge* (1958) that a positivist description of science ignores the role played by personal judgments.

Alfred Radcliffe-Brown (1881–1955) was an English social anthropologist who founded the Institute of Social and Cultural Anthropology at the University of Oxford. He was a structural-functionalist who carefully distinguished his own functionalist orientation from that of Bronislaw Malinowski.

Eugenio Rignano (1870–1930) was a philosopher whose book *The Psychology of Reasoning* (1923) influenced the young Evans-Pritchard. His predominant academic interest was in reconciling conflicting theories in science and philosophy.

Charles Seligman (1873–1940) was a British anthropologist at the London School of Economics in the early twentieth century. With his wife he conducted extensive survey research in the Southern Sudan, which influenced Edward Evans-Pritchard's decision to conduct work among the Azande.

Jonathan Spencer (b. 1954) is professor of anthropology at the University of Edinburgh. His research has concentrated on Sri Lanka and the relationship between politics and the state, while his textbook coauthored with Alan Barnard on anthropological theory and history is a resource widely read by undergraduates.

Paul Stoller (b. 1947) is professor of anthropology at the West Chester University of Pennsylvania. His research has focused on the anthropology of magic, religion, and the senses in West Africa, as well as economic and political anthropology among West African immigrants in New York City.

Keith Thomas (b. 1933) is a historian of the early modern period in British history. He is a Fellow of All Soul's College, University of Oxford, and is best known for his research on religion and magic.

C. Jason Throop is associate professor at the University of California at Los Angeles. He is a medical and psychological anthropologist whose research focuses on the cross-cultural phenomenology of pain, emotion, mood, and agency.

Victor Turner (1920–83) was a British anthropologist renowned for his work in symbolic anthropology. After training at the University of Manchester, his research focused on symbols, ritual, and rites of passage among the Ndembu in Zambia.

Edward Tylor (1832–1917) was considered the "father of anthropology," and developed an evolutionist theory of cultures. He is best known for his work *Primitive Culture: Researches into the Development of Mythology, Philosophy, Religion, Art, and Custom* (1871).

Harry West is a professor of anthropology at the School of Oriental and African Studies (SOAS), London. His research has focused on witchcraft, sorcery, and power among anticolonial rebels in Mozambique.

WORKS CITED

WORKS CITED

Ackerman, Robert. "Frazer, Sir James George (1854–1941)." In *Oxford Dictionary of National Biography*. Oxford: Oxford University Press, 2004. Accessed October 25, 2015. www.oxforddnb.com/view/article/33258.

Asad, Talal, ed. *Anthropology and the Colonial Encounter.* London: Ithaca Press, 1973.

Barnes, J. A. "Edward Evans-Pritchard: 1902–1973." *Proceedings of the British Academy* 73 (1987): 447–90.

Bartlett, Frederick. *Psychology and Primitive Culture.* Cambridge: Cambridge University Press, 1923.

Burton, John. "The Ghost of Malinowski in the Southern Sudan: Evans-Pritchard and Ethnographic Fieldwork." *Proceedings of the American Philosophical Society* 127, no. 4 (1983): 278–89.

Csordas, Thomas. "Morality as a Cultural System." *Current Anthropology* 54, no. 5 (2013): 523–46.

The Sacred Self. Berkeley: University of California Press, 1994.

Douglas, Mary. *Edward Evans-Pritchard.* London: Fontana, 1980.

"Thirty Years after Witchcraft, Oracles and Magic." In *Witchcraft Confessions and Accusations,* edited by Mary Douglas, xxi–xxxviii. London: Tavistock Publications, 1970.

Durkheim, Émile. *The Elementary Forms of Religious Life*. Translated by Karen Fields. London: Free Press, 1995.

Engelke, Matthew. "The Problem of Belief: Evans-Pritchard and Victor Turner on 'The Inner Life.'" *Anthropology Today* 18, no. 6 (2002): 3–8.

Evans-Pritchard, Edward. *The Azande: History and Political Institutions*. Oxford: Clarendon Press, 1971.

Essays in Social Anthropology. New York: Free Press of Glencoe, 1963.

"Genesis of a Social Anthropologist: An Autobiographical Note." *New Diffusionist* 3, no. 10 (1973): 17–23.

"The Intellectualist (English) Interpretation of Magic." *Bulletin of the Faculty of Arts* 1, Egyptian University, Cairo (1933): 282–311.

"The Intellectualist (English) Interpretation of Magic." *Journal of the Anthropological Society of Oxford* 4 (1973): 123–42.

"Lévy-Bruhl's Theory of Primitive Mentality." *Bulletin of the Faculty of Arts* 2, no. 2, Egyptian University, Cairo (1934): 1–36.

"The Morphology and Function of Magic: A Comparative Study of Trobriand and Zande Ritual and Spells." *American Anthropologist* 31, no. 4 (1929): 619–41.

Nuer Religion. Oxford: Clarendon Press, 1956.

"A Preliminary Account of the Ingassana Tribe in Fung Province." *Sudan Notes and Records* 10 (1927): 69–83.

"Social Anthropology at Oxford." *Man* 5, no. 4 (1970): 704.

Theories of Primitive Religion. Oxford: Clarendon Press, 1965.

"Witchcraft." *Africa* 8, no. 4 (1935): 417–22.

Witchcraft, Oracles, and Magic among the Azande. Oxford: Clarendon Press, 1937.

Witchcraft, Oracles, and Magic among the Azande. Oxford: Clarendon Press, 1976.

Favret-Saada, Jeanne. *Deadly Words: Witchcraft in the Bocage.* Cambridge: Cambridge University Press, 1980.

Fortes, Meyer. "An Anthropologist's Apprenticeship." *Annual Review of Anthropology* 7 (1978): 1–30.

Gellner, Ernest. Introduction to *A History of Anthropological Thought*, by Edward E. Evans-Pritchard. London: Faber and Faber, 1981.

Geschiere, Peter. *The Modernity of Witchcraft: Politics and the Occult in Postcolonial Africa.* Charlottesville and London: University Press of Virginia, 1997.

Gillies, Eva. Introduction to *Witchcraft, Oracles, and Magic among the Azande* by Edward E. Evans-Pritchard, viii–xxxiii. Oxford: Clarendon Press, 1976.

Goody, Jack. *The Domestication of the Savage Mind.* Cambridge: Cambridge University Press, 1977.

The Expansive Moment: The Rise of Social Anthropology in Britain and Africa 1918–1970. Cambridge: Cambridge University Press, 1995.

Hsu, Elisabeth. *The Transmission of Chinese Medicine.* Cambridge: Cambridge University Press, 1999.

Jacobs, Struan. "Two Sources of Michael Polanyi's Prototypal Notion of incommensurability: Evans-Pritchard on Azande Witchcraft and St.

Augustine on Conversion." *History of the Human Sciences* 16, no. 2 (2003): 57–76.

Lévy-Bruhl, Lucien. *How Natives Think*. Translated by Lilian A. Clare. Princeton: Princeton University Press, 1985.

Lock, Margaret and Patricia Kaufert, eds. *Pragmatic Women and Body Politics*. Cambridge: Cambridge University Press, 1998.

Luhrmann, Tanya. *Of Two Minds: The Growing Disorder in American Psychiatry*. London: Picador, 2000.

Persuasions of the Witch's Craft: Ritual Magic and Witchcraft in Present-Day England. Oxford: Basil Blackwell, 1989.

"What Anthropology Should Learn from G. E. R. Lloyd." *Journal of Ethnographic Theory* 3, no. 1 (2013): 171–3.

When God Talks Back: Understanding the American Evangelical Relationship with God. New York: Albert Knopf, 2012.

Lutz, Catherine. "The Anthropology of Emotions." *Annual Review of Anthropology* 15 (1986): 405–36.

Macfarlane, Alan. *Witchcraft in Tudor and Stuart England: A Regional and Comparative Study*. London: Routledge and Kegan Paul, 1970.

Malinowski, Bronislaw. *Argonauts of the Western Pacific*. London: Routledge and Kegan Paul, 1922.

Marwick, M. G. *Sorcery in its Social Setting: A Study of the Northern Rhodesian Cewa*. Manchester: Manchester University Press, 1965.

Mayer, P. "Witches." Inaugural Lecture, Rhodes University, Grahamstown, 1954.

Meyer, Birgit, and Peter Pels, eds. *Magic and Modernity: Interfaces of Revelation and Concealment*. Stanford: Stanford University Press, 2003.

Mills, Martin. "The Opposite of Witchcraft: Evans-Pritchard and the Problem of the Person." *Journal of the Royal Anthropological Institute* 19, no. 1 (2013): 18–33.

Mitchell, J. Clyde. *The Yao Village: A Study in the Social Structure of a Nyasaland Tribe*. Manchester: Manchester University Press, 1956.

Mol, Annemarie. *The Body Multiple: Ontology in Medical Practice*. Durham, North Carolina: Duke University Press, 2002.

Morton, Christopher. "Evans-Pritchard and Malinowski: The Roots of a Complex Relationship." *History of Anthropology Newsletter* 34, no. 2 (2007): 10–14.

Murphy, Keith M., and C. Jason Throop. *Toward an Anthropology of the Will*. Stanford: Stanford University Press, 2010.

Polanyi, Michael. *Personal Knowledge: Towards a Post-Critical Philosophy*.

London: Routledge & Kegan Paul, 1958.

Spencer, Jonathan, and Alan Bernard. "Functionalism" and "The Politics of Knowledge." In *The Routledge Encyclopedia of Social and Cultural Anthropology.* London: Routledge, 2010. Accessed October 25, 2015. eBook Collection (EBSCOhost).

Stoller, Paul. *Fusion of the Worlds: An Ethnography of Possession Among the Songhay of Niger.* Chicago: University of Chicago Press, 1989.

Turner, Victor. *Schism and Continuity in an African Society: A Study of Ndembu Village Life.* Manchester: Manchester University Press for Rhodes Livingstone Institute, 1957.

Tylor, Edward. "On the Survival of Savage Thought in Modern Civilization." *Proceedings of the Royal Institute* (1869).

West, Harry. *Ethnographic Sorcery.* Chicago: University of Chicago Press, 2008.

Kupilikula: Governance and the Invisible Realm in Mozambique. Chicago: University of Chicago Press, 2005.

THE MACAT LIBRARY
BY DISCIPLINE

AFRICANA STUDIES

Chinua Achebe's *An Image of Africa: Racism in Conrad's Heart of Darkness*
W. E. B. Du Bois's *The Souls of Black Folk*
Zora Neale Huston's *Characteristics of Negro Expression*
Martin Luther King Jr's *Why We Can't Wait*
Toni Morrison's *Playing in the Dark: Whiteness in the American Literary Imagination*

ANTHROPOLOGY

Arjun Appadurai's *Modernity at Large: Cultural Dimensions of Globalisation*
Philippe Ariès's *Centuries of Childhood*
Franz Boas's *Race, Language and Culture*
Kim Chan & Renée Mauborgne's *Blue Ocean Strategy*
Jared Diamond's *Guns, Germs & Steel: the Fate of Human Societies*
Jared Diamond's *Collapse: How Societies Choose to Fail or Survive*
E. E. Evans-Pritchard's *Witchcraft, Oracles and Magic Among the Azande*
James Ferguson's *The Anti-Politics Machine*
Clifford Geertz's *The Interpretation of Cultures*
David Graeber's *Debt: the First 5000 Years*
Karen Ho's *Liquidated: An Ethnography of Wall Street*
Geert Hofstede's *Culture's Consequences: Comparing Values, Behaviors, Institutes and Organizations across Nations*
Claude Lévi-Strauss's *Structural Anthropology*
Jay Macleod's *Ain't No Makin' It: Aspirations and Attainment in a Low-Income Neighborhood*
Saba Mahmood's *The Politics of Piety: The Islamic Revival and the Feminist Subject*
Marcel Mauss's *The Gift*

BUSINESS

Jean Lave & Etienne Wenger's *Situated Learning*
Theodore Levitt's *Marketing Myopia*
Burton G. Malkiel's *A Random Walk Down Wall Street*
Douglas McGregor's *The Human Side of Enterprise*
Michael Porter's *Competitive Strategy: Creating and Sustaining Superior Performance*
John Kotter's *Leading Change*
C. K. Prahalad & Gary Hamel's *The Core Competence of the Corporation*

CRIMINOLOGY

Michelle Alexander's *The New Jim Crow: Mass Incarceration in the Age of Colorblindness*
Michael R. Gottfredson & Travis Hirschi's *A General Theory of Crime*
Richard Herrnstein & Charles A. Murray's *The Bell Curve: Intelligence and Class Structure in American Life*
Elizabeth Loftus's *Eyewitness Testimony*
Jay Macleod's *Ain't No Makin' It: Aspirations and Attainment in a Low-Income Neighborhood*
Philip Zimbardo's *The Lucifer Effect*

ECONOMICS

Janet Abu-Lughod's *Before European Hegemony*
Ha-Joon Chang's *Kicking Away the Ladder*
David Brion Davis's *The Problem of Slavery in the Age of Revolution*
Milton Friedman's *The Role of Monetary Policy*
Milton Friedman's *Capitalism and Freedom*
David Graeber's *Debt: the First 5000 Years*
Friedrich Hayek's *The Road to Serfdom*
Karen Ho's *Liquidated: An Ethnography of Wall Street*

The Macat Library By Discipline

John Maynard Keynes's *The General Theory of Employment, Interest and Money*
Charles P. Kindleberger's *Manias, Panics and Crashes*
Robert Lucas's *Why Doesn't Capital Flow from Rich to Poor Countries?*
Burton G. Malkiel's *A Random Walk Down Wall Street*
Thomas Robert Malthus's *An Essay on the Principle of Population*
Karl Marx's *Capital*
Thomas Piketty's *Capital in the Twenty-First Century*
Amartya Sen's *Development as Freedom*
Adam Smith's *The Wealth of Nations*
Nassim Nicholas Taleb's *The Black Swan: The Impact of the Highly Improbable*
Amos Tversky's & Daniel Kahneman's *Judgment under Uncertainty: Heuristics and Biases*
Mahbub Ul Haq's *Reflections on Human Development*
Max Weber's *The Protestant Ethic and the Spirit of Capitalism*

FEMINISM AND GENDER STUDIES

Judith Butler's *Gender Trouble*
Simone De Beauvoir's *The Second Sex*
Michel Foucault's *History of Sexuality*
Betty Friedan's *The Feminine Mystique*
Saba Mahmood's *The Politics of Piety: The Islamic Revival and the Feminist Subjec*t
Joan Wallach Scott's *Gender and the Politics of History*
Mary Wollstonecraft's *A Vindication of the Rights of Woman*
Virginia Woolf's *A Room of One's Own*

GEOGRAPHY

The Brundtland Report's *Our Common Future*
Rachel Carson's *Silent Spring*
Charles Darwin's *On the Origin of Species*
James Ferguson's *The Anti-Politics Machine*
Jane Jacobs's *The Death and Life of Great American Cities*
James Lovelock's *Gaia: A New Look at Life on Earth*
Amartya Sen's *Development as Freedom*
Mathis Wackernagel & William Rees's *Our Ecological Footprint*

HISTORY

Janet Abu-Lughod's *Before European Hegemony*
Benedict Anderson's *Imagined Communities*
Bernard Bailyn's *The Ideological Origins of the American Revolution*
Hanna Batatu's *The Old Social Classes And The Revolutionary Movements Of Iraq*
Christopher Browning's *Ordinary Men: Reserve Police Batallion 101 and the Final Solution in Poland*
Edmund Burke's *Reflections on the Revolution in France*
William Cronon's *Nature's Metropolis: Chicago And The Great West*
Alfred W. Crosby's *The Columbian Exchange*
Hamid Dabashi's *Iran: A People Interrupted*
David Brion Davis's *The Problem of Slavery in the Age of Revolution*
Nathalie Zemon Davis's *The Return of Martin Guerre*
Jared Diamond's *Guns, Germs & Steel: the Fate of Human Societies*
Frank Dikotter's *Mao's Great Famine*
John W Dower's *War Without Mercy: Race And Power In The Pacific War*
W. E. B. Du Bois's *The Souls of Black Folk*
Richard J. Evans's *In Defence of History*
Lucien Febvre's *The Problem of Unbelief in the 16th Century*
Sheila Fitzpatrick's *Everyday Stalinism*

Eric Foner's *Reconstruction: America's Unfinished Revolution, 1863-1877*
Michel Foucault's *Discipline and Punish*
Michel Foucault's *History of Sexuality*
Francis Fukuyama's *The End of History and the Last Man*
John Lewis Gaddis's *We Now Know: Rethinking Cold War History*
Ernest Gellner's *Nations and Nationalism*
Eugene Genovese's *Roll, Jordan, Roll: The World the Slaves Made*
Carlo Ginzburg's *The Night Battles*
Daniel Goldhagen's *Hitler's Willing Executioners*
Jack Goldstone's *Revolution and Rebellion in the Early Modern World*
Antonio Gramsci's *The Prison Notebooks*
Alexander Hamilton, John Jay & James Madison's *The Federalist Papers*
Christopher Hill's *The World Turned Upside Down*
Carole Hillenbrand's *The Crusades: Islamic Perspectives*
Thomas Hobbes's *Leviathan*
Eric Hobsbawm's *The Age Of Revolution*
John A. Hobson's *Imperialism: A Study*
Albert Hourani's *History of the Arab Peoples*
Samuel P. Huntington's *The Clash of Civilizations and the Remaking of World Order*
C. L. R. James's *The Black Jacobins*
Tony Judt's *Postwar: A History of Europe Since 1945*
Ernst Kantorowicz's *The King's Two Bodies: A Study in Medieval Political Theology*
Paul Kennedy's *The Rise and Fall of the Great Powers*
Ian Kershaw's *The "Hitler Myth": Image and Reality in the Third Reich*
John Maynard Keynes's *The General Theory of Employment, Interest and Money*
Charles P. Kindleberger's *Manias, Panics and Crashes*
Martin Luther King Jr's *Why We Can't Wait*
Henry Kissinger's *World Order: Reflections on the Character of Nations and the Course of History*
Thomas Kuhn's *The Structure of Scientific Revolutions*
Georges Lefebvre's *The Coming of the French Revolution*
John Locke's *Two Treatises of Government*
Niccolò Machiavelli's *The Prince*
Thomas Robert Malthus's *An Essay on the Principle of Population*
Mahmood Mamdani's *Citizen and Subject: Contemporary Africa And The Legacy Of Late Colonialism*
Karl Marx's *Capital*
Stanley Milgram's *Obedience to Authority*
John Stuart Mill's *On Liberty*
Thomas Paine's *Common Sense*
Thomas Paine's *Rights of Man*
Geoffrey Parker's *Global Crisis: War, Climate Change and Catastrophe in the Seventeenth Century*
Jonathan Riley-Smith's *The First Crusade and the Idea of Crusading*
Jean-Jacques Rousseau's *The Social Contract*
Joan Wallach Scott's *Gender and the Politics of History*
Theda Skocpol's *States and Social Revolutions*
Adam Smith's *The Wealth of Nations*
Timothy Snyder's *Bloodlands: Europe Between Hitler and Stalin*
Sun Tzu's *The Art of War*
Keith Thomas's *Religion and the Decline of Magic*
Thucydides's *The History of the Peloponnesian War*
Frederick Jackson Turner's *The Significance of the Frontier in American History*
Odd Arne Westad's *The Global Cold War: Third World Interventions And The Making Of Our Times*

The Macat Library By Discipline

LITERATURE

Chinua Achebe's *An Image of Africa: Racism in Conrad's Heart of Darkness*
Roland Barthes's *Mythologies*
Homi K. Bhabha's *The Location of Culture*
Judith Butler's *Gender Trouble*
Simone De Beauvoir's *The Second Sex*
Ferdinand De Saussure's *Course in General Linguistics*
T. S. Eliot's *The Sacred Wood: Essays on Poetry and Criticism*
Zora Neale Huston's *Characteristics of Negro Expression*
Toni Morrison's *Playing in the Dark: Whiteness in the American Literary Imagination*
Edward Said's *Orientalism*
Gayatri Chakravorty Spivak's *Can the Subaltern Speak?*
Mary Wollstonecraft's *A Vindication of the Rights of Women*
Virginia Woolf's *A Room of One's Own*

PHILOSOPHY

Elizabeth Anscombe's *Modern Moral Philosophy*
Hannah Arendt's *The Human Condition*
Aristotle's *Metaphysics*
Aristotle's *Nicomachean Ethics*
Edmund Gettier's *Is Justified True Belief Knowledge?*
Georg Wilhelm Friedrich Hegel's *Phenomenology of Spirit*
David Hume's *Dialogues Concerning Natural Religion*
David Hume's *The Enquiry for Human Understanding*
Immanuel Kant's *Religion within the Boundaries of Mere Reason*
Immanuel Kant's *Critique of Pure Reason*
Søren Kierkegaard's *The Sickness Unto Death*
Søren Kierkegaard's *Fear and Trembling*
C. S. Lewis's *The Abolition of Man*
Alasdair MacIntyre's *After Virtue*
Marcus Aurelius's *Meditations*
Friedrich Nietzsche's *On the Genealogy of Morality*
Friedrich Nietzsche's *Beyond Good and Evil*
Plato's *Republic*
Plato's *Symposium*
Jean-Jacques Rousseau's *The Social Contract*
Gilbert Ryle's *The Concept of Mind*
Baruch Spinoza's *Ethics*
Sun Tzu's *The Art of War*
Ludwig Wittgenstein's *Philosophical Investigations*

POLITICS

Benedict Anderson's *Imagined Communities*
Aristotle's *Politics*
Bernard Bailyn's *The Ideological Origins of the American Revolution*
Edmund Burke's *Reflections on the Revolution in France*
John C. Calhoun's *A Disquisition on Government*
Ha-Joon Chang's *Kicking Away the Ladder*
Hamid Dabashi's *Iran: A People Interrupted*
Hamid Dabashi's *Theology of Discontent: The Ideological Foundation of the Islamic Revolution in Iran*
Robert Dahl's *Democracy and its Critics*
Robert Dahl's *Who Governs?*
David Brion Davis's *The Problem of Slavery in the Age of Revolution*

Alexis De Tocqueville's *Democracy in America*
James Ferguson's *The Anti-Politics Machine*
Frank Dikotter's *Mao's Great Famine*
Sheila Fitzpatrick's *Everyday Stalinism*
Eric Foner's *Reconstruction: America's Unfinished Revolution, 1863-1877*
Milton Friedman's *Capitalism and Freedom*
Francis Fukuyama's *The End of History and the Last Man*
John Lewis Gaddis's *We Now Know: Rethinking Cold War History*
Ernest Gellner's *Nations and Nationalism*
David Graeber's *Debt: the First 5000 Years*
Antonio Gramsci's *The Prison Notebooks*
Alexander Hamilton, John Jay & James Madison's *The Federalist Papers*
Friedrich Hayek's *The Road to Serfdom*
Christopher Hill's *The World Turned Upside Down*
Thomas Hobbes's *Leviathan*
John A. Hobson's *Imperialism: A Study*
Samuel P. Huntington's *The Clash of Civilizations and the Remaking of World Order*
Tony Judt's *Postwar: A History of Europe Since 1945*
David C. Kang's *China Rising: Peace, Power and Order in East Asia*
Paul Kennedy's *The Rise and Fall of Great Powers*
Robert Keohane's *After Hegemony*
Martin Luther King Jr.'s *Why We Can't Wait*
Henry Kissinger's *World Order: Reflections on the Character of Nations and the Course of History*
John Locke's *Two Treatises of Government*
Niccolò Machiavelli's *The Prince*
Thomas Robert Malthus's *An Essay on the Principle of Population*
Mahmood Mamdani's *Citizen and Subject: Contemporary Africa And The Legacy Of Late Colonialism*
Karl Marx's *Capital*
John Stuart Mill's *On Liberty*
John Stuart Mill's *Utilitarianism*
Hans Morgenthau's *Politics Among Nations*
Thomas Paine's *Common Sense*
Thomas Paine's *Rights of Man*
Thomas Piketty's *Capital in the Twenty-First Century*
Robert D. Putman's *Bowling Alone*
John Rawls's *Theory of Justice*
Jean-Jacques Rousseau's *The Social Contract*
Theda Skocpol's *States and Social Revolutions*
Adam Smith's *The Wealth of Nations*
Sun Tzu's *The Art of War*
Henry David Thoreau's *Civil Disobedience*
Thucydides's *The History of the Peloponnesian War*
Kenneth Waltz's *Theory of International Politics*
Max Weber's *Politics as a Vocation*
Odd Arne Westad's *The Global Cold War: Third World Interventions And The Making Of Our Times*

POSTCOLONIAL STUDIES

Roland Barthes's *Mythologies*
Frantz Fanon's *Black Skin, White Masks*
Homi K. Bhabha's *The Location of Culture*
Gustavo Gutiérrez's *A Theology of Liberation*
Edward Said's *Orientalism*
Gayatri Chakravorty Spivak's *Can the Subaltern Speak?*

PSYCHOLOGY

Gordon Allport's *The Nature of Prejudice*
Alan Baddeley & Graham Hitch's *Aggression: A Social Learning Analysis*
Albert Bandura's *Aggression: A Social Learning Analysis*
Leon Festinger's *A Theory of Cognitive Dissonance*
Sigmund Freud's *The Interpretation of Dreams*
Betty Friedan's *The Feminine Mystique*
Michael R. Gottfredson & Travis Hirschi's *A General Theory of Crime*
Eric Hoffer's *The True Believer: Thoughts on the Nature of Mass Movements*
William James's *Principles of Psychology*
Elizabeth Loftus's *Eyewitness Testimony*
A. H. Maslow's *A Theory of Human Motivation*
Stanley Milgram's *Obedience to Authority*
Steven Pinker's *The Better Angels of Our Nature*
Oliver Sacks's *The Man Who Mistook His Wife For a Hat*
Richard Thaler & Cass Sunstein's *Nudge: Improving Decisions About Health, Wealth and Happiness*
Amos Tversky's *Judgment under Uncertainty: Heuristics and Biases*
Philip Zimbardo's *The Lucifer Effect*

SCIENCE

Rachel Carson's *Silent Spring*
William Cronon's *Nature's Metropolis: Chicago And The Great West*
Alfred W. Crosby's *The Columbian Exchange*
Charles Darwin's *On the Origin of Species*
Richard Dawkin's *The Selfish Gene*
Thomas Kuhn's *The Structure of Scientific Revolutions*
Geoffrey Parker's *Global Crisis: War, Climate Change and Catastrophe in the Seventeenth Century*
Mathis Wackernagel & William Rees's *Our Ecological Footprint*

SOCIOLOGY

Michelle Alexander's *The New Jim Crow: Mass Incarceration in the Age of Colorblindness*
Gordon Allport's *The Nature of Prejudice*
Albert Bandura's *Aggression: A Social Learning Analysis*
Hanna Batatu's *The Old Social Classes And The Revolutionary Movements Of Iraq*
Ha-Joon Chang's *Kicking Away the Ladder*
W. E. B. Du Bois's *The Souls of Black Folk*
Émile Durkheim's *On Suicide*
Frantz Fanon's *Black Skin, White Masks*
Frantz Fanon's *The Wretched of the Earth*
Eric Foner's *Reconstruction: America's Unfinished Revolution, 1863-1877*
Eugene Genovese's *Roll, Jordan, Roll: The World the Slaves Made*
Jack Goldstone's *Revolution and Rebellion in the Early Modern World*
Antonio Gramsci's *The Prison Notebooks*
Richard Herrnstein & Charles A Murray's *The Bell Curve: Intelligence and Class Structure in American Life*
Eric Hoffer's *The True Believer: Thoughts on the Nature of Mass Movements*
Jane Jacobs's *The Death and Life of Great American Cities*
Robert Lucas's *Why Doesn't Capital Flow from Rich to Poor Countries?*
Jay Macleod's *Ain't No Makin' It: Aspirations and Attainment in a Low Income Neighborhood*
Elaine May's *Homeward Bound: American Families in the Cold War Era*
Douglas McGregor's *The Human Side of Enterprise*
C. Wright Mills's *The Sociological Imagination*

Thomas Piketty's *Capital in the Twenty-First Century*
Robert D. Putman's *Bowling Alone*
David Riesman's *The Lonely Crowd: A Study of the Changing American Character*
Edward Said's *Orientalism*
Joan Wallach Scott's *Gender and the Politics of History*
Theda Skocpol's *States and Social Revolutions*
Max Weber's *The Protestant Ethic and the Spirit of Capitalism*

THEOLOGY

Augustine's *Confessions*
Benedict's *Rule of St Benedict*
Gustavo Gutiérrez's *A Theology of Liberation*
Carole Hillenbrand's *The Crusades: Islamic Perspectives*
David Hume's *Dialogues Concerning Natural Religion*
Immanuel Kant's *Religion within the Boundaries of Mere Reason*
Ernst Kantorowicz's *The King's Two Bodies: A Study in Medieval Political Theology*
Søren Kierkegaard's *The Sickness Unto Death*
C. S. Lewis's *The Abolition of Man*
Saba Mahmood's *The Politics of Piety: The Islamic Revival and the Feminist Subject*
Baruch Spinoza's *Ethics*
Keith Thomas's *Religion and the Decline of Magic*

COMING SOON

Chris Argyris's *The Individual and the Organisation*
Seyla Benhabib's *The Rights of Others*
Walter Benjamin's *The Work Of Art in the Age of Mechanical Reproduction*
John Berger's *Ways of Seeing*
Pierre Bourdieu's *Outline of a Theory of Practice*
Mary Douglas's *Purity and Danger*
Roland Dworkin's *Taking Rights Seriously*
James G. March's *Exploration and Exploitation in Organisational Learning*
Ikujiro Nonaka's *A Dynamic Theory of Organizational Knowledge Creation*
Griselda Pollock's *Vision and Difference*
Amartya Sen's *Inequality Re-Examined*
Susan Sontag's *On Photography*
Yasser Tabbaa's *The Transformation of Islamic Art*
Ludwig von Mises's *Theory of Money and Credit*

Macat Disciplines

Access the greatest ideas and thinkers across entire disciplines, including

FEMINISM, GENDER AND QUEER STUDIES

Simone De Beauvoir's
The Second Sex

Michel Foucault's
History of Sexuality

Betty Friedan's
The Feminine Mystique

Saba Mahmood's
*The Politics of Piety:
The Islamic Revival and
the Feminist Subject*

Joan Wallach Scott's
*Gender and the
Politics of History*

Mary Wollstonecraft's
*A Vindication of the
Rights of Woman*

Virginia Woolf's
A Room of One's Own

Judith Butler's
Gender Trouble

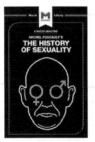

Macat analyses are available from all good bookshops and libraries.

Access hundreds of analyses through one, multimedia tool.

Join free for one month **library.macat.com**

Macat Disciplines

Access the greatest ideas and thinkers across entire disciplines, including

CRIMINOLOGY

Michelle Alexander's
The New Jim Crow:
Mass Incarceration in the
Age of Colorblindness

Michael R. Gottfredson
& Travis Hirschi's
A General Theory of Crime

Elizabeth Loftus's
Eyewitness Testimony

Richard Herrnstein
& Charles A. Murray's
The Bell Curve: Intelligence and
Class Structure in American Life

Jay Macleod's
Ain't No Makin' It:
Aspirations and Attainment in a
Low-Income Neighborhood

Philip Zimbardo's
The Lucifer Effect

Macat analyses are available from all good bookshops and libraries.

Access hundreds of analyses through one, multimedia tool.

Join free for one month **library.macat.com**

Macat Disciplines

Access the greatest ideas and thinkers across entire disciplines, including

MAN AND THE ENVIRONMENT

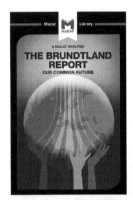

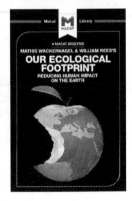

The Brundtland Report's, *Our Common Future*
Rachel Carson's, *Silent Spring*
James Lovelock's, *Gaia: A New Look at Life on Earth*
Mathis Wackernagel & William Rees's, *Our Ecological Footprint*

Macat analyses are available from all good bookshops and libraries.

Access hundreds of analyses through one, multimedia tool.
Join free for one month **library.macat.com**

  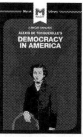 

Macat Disciplines

Access the greatest ideas and thinkers across entire disciplines, including

TOTALITARIANISM

Sheila Fitzpatrick's, *Everyday Stalinism*
Ian Kershaw's, *The "Hitler Myth"*
Timothy Snyder's, *Bloodlands*

Macat Pairs

*Analyse historical and modern issues
from opposite sides of an argument.
Pairs include:*

RACE AND IDENTITY

Zora Neale Hurston's
Characteristics of Negro Expression

Using material collected on anthropological expeditions to the South, Zora Neale Hurston explains how expression in African American culture in the early twentieth century departs from the art of white America. At the time, African American art was often criticized for copying white culture. For Hurston, this criticism misunderstood how art works. European tradition views art as something fixed. But Hurston describes a creative process that is alive, ever-changing, and largely improvisational. She maintains that African American art works through a process called 'mimicry'—where an imitated object or verbal pattern, for example, is reshaped and altered until it becomes something new, novel—and worthy of attention.

Frantz Fanon's
Black Skin, White Masks

Black Skin, White Masks offers a radical analysis of the psychological effects of colonization on the colonized.

Fanon witnessed the effects of colonization first hand both in his birthplace, Martinique, and again later in life when he worked as a psychiatrist in another French colony, Algeria. His text is uncompromising in form and argument. He dissects the dehumanizing effects of colonialism, arguing that it destroys the native sense of identity, forcing people to adapt to an alien set of values—including a core belief that they are inferior. This results in deep psychological trauma.

Fanon's work played a pivotal role in the civil rights movements of the 1960s.

Macat analyses are available from all good bookshops and libraries.

Access hundreds of analyses through one, multimedia tool.
Join free for one month **library.macat.com**

Macat Pairs

Analyse historical and modern issues from opposite sides of an argument. Pairs include:

ARE WE FUNDAMENTALLY GOOD - OR BAD?

Steven Pinker's
The Better Angels of Our Nature

Stephen Pinker's gloriously optimistic 2011 book argues that, despite humanity's biological tendency toward violence, we are, in fact, less violent today than ever before. To prove his case, Pinker lays out pages of detailed statistical evidence. For him, much of the credit for the decline goes to the eighteenth-century Enlightenment movement, whose ideas of liberty, tolerance, and respect for the value of human life filtered down through society and affected how people thought. That psychological change led to behavioral change—and overall we became more peaceful. Critics countered that humanity could never overcome the biological urge toward violence; others argued that Pinker's statistics were flawed.

Philip Zimbardo's
The Lucifer Effect

Some psychologists believe those who commit cruelty are innately evil. Zimbardo disagrees. In *The Lucifer Effect*, he argues that sometimes good people do evil things simply because of the situations they find themselves in, citing many historical examples to illustrate his point. Zimbardo details his 1971 Stanford prison experiment, where ordinary volunteers playing guards in a mock prison rapidly became abusive. But he also describes the tortures committed by US army personnel in Iraq's Abu Ghraib prison in 2003—and how he himself testified in defence of one of those guards. committed by US army personnel in Iraq's Abu Ghraib prison in 2003—and how he himself testified in defence of one of those guards.

Macat analyses are available from all good bookshops and libraries.

Access hundreds of analyses through one, multimedia tool.

Join free for one month **library.macat.com**

Macat Pairs

*Analyse historical and modern issues
from opposite sides of an argument.
Pairs include:*

HOW WE RELATE TO EACH OTHER AND SOCIETY

Jean-Jacques Rousseau's
The Social Contract

Rousseau's famous work sets out the radical concept of the 'social contract': a give-and-take relationship between individual freedom and social order.

If people are free to do as they like, governed only by their own sense of justice, they are also vulnerable to chaos and violence. To avoid this, Rousseau proposes, they should agree to give up some freedom to benefit from the protection of social and political organization. But this deal is only just if societies are led by the collective needs and desires of the people, and able to control the private interests of individuals. For Rousseau, the only legitimate form of government is rule by the people.

Robert D. Putnam's
Bowling Alone

In *Bowling Alone*, Robert Putnam argues that Americans have become disconnected from one another and from the institutions of their common life, and investigates the consequences of this change.

Looking at a range of indicators, from membership in formal organizations to the number of invitations being extended to informal dinner parties, Putnam demonstrates that Americans are interacting less and creating less "social capital" – with potentially disastrous implications for their society.

It would be difficult to overstate the impact of *Bowling Alone*, one of the most frequently cited social science publications of the last half-century.

Printed in the United States
by Baker & Taylor Publisher Services